HOW TO HANDLE TOUGH SITUATIONS AT WORK

Books to make you better

Books to make you better. To make you *be* better, *do* better, *feel* better. Whether you want to upgrade your personal skills or change your job, whether you want to improve your managerial style, become a more powerful communicator, or be stimulated and inspired as you work.

Prentice Hall Business is leading the field with a new breed of skills, careers and development books. Books that are a cut above the mainstream – in topic, content and delivery – with an edge and verve that will make you better, with less effort.

Books that are as sharp and smart as you are.

Prentice Hall Business.
We work harder – so you don't have to.

For more details on products, and to contact us, visit
www.business-minds.com
www.yourmomentum.com

HOW TO HANDLE TOUGH SITUATIONS AT WORK

A manager's guide to over
100 testing situations

ROS JAY

Prentice
Hall

BUSINESS

An imprint of **Pearson Education**

London • New York • Toronto • Sydney • Tokyo • Singapore • Hong Kong • Cape Town

New Delhi • Madrid • Paris • Amsterdam • Munich • Milan • Stockholm

PEARSON EDUCATION LIMITED

Head Office:
Edinburgh Gate
Harlow CM20 2JE
Tel: +44 (0)1279 623623
Fax: +44 (0)1279 431059

London Office:
128 Long Acre
London WC2E 9AN
Tel: +44 (0)20 7447 2000
Fax: +44 (0)20 7447 2170
Websites: www.business-minds.com
www.yourmomentum.com

_____

First published in Great Britain in 2003

© Pearson Education 2003

The right of Ros Jay to be identified as author
of this work has been asserted by her in accordance
with the Copyright, Designs and Patents Act 1988

ISBN 0 273 65603 1

British Library Cataloguing in Publication Data
A CIP catalogue record for this book can be obtained from the British Library

10 9 8 7 6 5 4 3 2

Typeset by Northern Phototypesetting Co. Ltd, Bolton
Printed and bound in Great Britain by Bell & Bain Ltd, Glasgow

The publishers' policy is to use paper manufactured from sustainable forests.

Contents

2 Your managers   109

3 Colleagues   145

Introduction

Every so often a problem comes along that makes your stomach sink. How on earth are you going to handle it? There are some really tough situations, and the reason you don't know how to handle them is because no one ever told you. Until now.

We all find some parts of our job harder to do than others. And we all have tasks that we don't particularly enjoy – such as disciplining people, drawing up budgets or writing reports. But these aren't really tough; they're just unpleasant. It's not that you don't know *how* to handle them; you just don't *want* to do it.

The really tough situations are the ones that you haven't encountered before, and which aren't in the training manuals. For example, what if your boss tries to blame you for their mistake? Or you have to discipline a team member who is also a friend? Or you think a customer is lying to you? Or you're asked to justify what you know deep down is a bad decision?

Where are you supposed to go for help in these situations? Until now, there really wasn't an easy answer. *How to handle tough situations at work* is designed to change all that. You see, *you* may not have encountered these situations before but other people have. And that means they've found out the answers – they just haven't told you. That's what this book is here for. With solutions to over a hundred tough situations, you'll find answers to pretty well all your knottiest problems. You may not relish carrying some of them out; others will be enjoyable. All of them will be effective. And, however you feel about them, at least you'll know what you're doing and why. So the situation may call for courage, diplomacy, skill or patience. It may be difficult or it may be easy. But it will no longer be tough.

CHAPTER 1

YOUR TEAM

Your team is worried about threatened redundancies

You presumably can't prevent the redundancies, so the way to keep this crisis to a minimum is to handle it sensitively, and to recognize that even those people who are not made redundant will feel threatened – next time it could be them, after all.

- Keep everyone fully informed from the earliest stage possible. Don't wait until you have more information. People always get wind of trouble, and their imaginations will blow it up into something bigger than it really is, so you're not protecting them by keeping quiet.

- Don't just tell them the basics – tell them whatever they want to know. How many redundancies? What departments? What are the criteria for deciding who should go?

- Don't, however, give them guesses. If you haven't got the information you can try to find out, but don't speculate. They'll take whatever you say to them as gospel, having nothing else to go on.

You've been told you have to make redundancies in your department

It is critical that you can justify your method of selecting people for redundancy. You absolutely don't want to be – or even appear to be – guilty of bias. So you need to apply an unemotional approach to what is, of course, a very emotive issue. Selecting people for redundancy is a harrowing task so, for both legal and personal reasons, you need to be sure you're being scrupulously fair.

You need to balance up the factors that you can legitimately take into account when laying people off. So you need to know what constitutes reasonable grounds. There are some factors that you can consider:

- Length of service – you should certainly take this into account, and you may use it as your only criterion – 'last in, first out'.

- Pay – assuming that finances are a key reason for redundancies, you could reasonably argue that the most expensive personnel should go. However, these are often the longest serving people and long service is a good criterion for hanging on to someone. The best solution is to offer your longest serving staff the chance to stay if they will take a cut in pay.

- Skills – if someone's skills, or lack of them, are relevant to the redundancy, it can justify laying them off. But if their skills don't impinge in any way, it won't constitute grounds for redundancy.

- Performance – this is a fair consideration, but you have to be able to give a clear and relevant demonstration that a person's performance is poor.

- Attendance/discipline – you can generally justify selecting someone for redundancy if their attendance record is poor (but take the reason for this into account) or if they have a poor disciplinary record.

- Loyalty – poor loyalty can sometimes be enough reason to select someone. For example, if the need for redundancies was caused in part by a strike, you could justify selecting a worker who went on strike over one who didn't.

Think about redundancy from the point of view of the people who get laid off for a moment. They may be left without a job for a while, which means that they will struggle to pay the mortgage, the loan on the car and the children's school fees. If they manage to get another job it could mean a cut in salary, or it might mean relocating – that means moving house so maybe their partner will have to change jobs too, and the kids will have to change schools.

The very least someone facing this needs is to be given as much notice as possible. In unionized organizations, management consult with the unions before confirming any redundancies. In non-unionized organizations this doesn't always happen. There may be unofficial rumours, but the first anyone knows for sure is when you call them in and tell them that they don't have a job any more. Clearly this is unreasonable. People need to know if there is a threat of redundancy so that they can plan their options in good time in case they are one of the ones made redundant. So call your team together as soon as you have any firm information. Even if it's inconclusive, at least tell them what you can. It might be, 'We're going to have to make between two and four redundancies in this department, and the final decisions won't be taken until the end of July.' Let them see that you are sympathetic and will do everything you can to keep them informed as the process continues.

> "Once you have decided to make someone redundant, you will have to tell them. The only way to do this is face-to-face".

Breaking the news

Once you have decided to make someone redundant, you will have to tell them. The only way to do this is face-to-face and, apart from any official communications with your own managers, the person you're telling must be the first person to know. Imagine how they would feel if rumours got out that they were being made redundant before they'd heard it officially from you. There are some things you should consider when preparing to talk to them.

- Find a relaxed and private opportunity to talk to the person. Don't sit across a desk in manager/subordinate style, but try to find somewhere that you can have a cup of coffee together.

- Having prepared the ground your employee will no doubt have guessed what they are there for. Tell them straight, expressing sympathy and reassuring them that you appreciate their input into the organization and will be very sorry to lose them.

- Find something specific to praise about their performance. This should be far more sincere than a glib, 'You've worked hard.' Something such as, 'I'll miss your attention to detail when we're planning projects,' or 'Everyone appreciates your cheerful enthusiasm, and there'll be a gap when you've gone.' Redundancy knocks a person's self-esteem, so make an effort to keep theirs as intact as possible.

- They may want to talk about it, argue about it or may even burst into tears. Let them express their feelings, so long as they don't become aggressive, without feeling you want to rush them out of the office. (Make sure you have a box of tissues handy.)

- If they want to know why they were selected for redundancy, tell them. They are entitled to know. If you've been scrupulously fair about the process, they should see the logic – even if they're not happy about it.

You are legally obliged to put the dismissal in writing. However, just because this is a legal requirement, it doesn't mean that it's OK to write a sterile and unfeeling letter. As well as stating the necessary facts, you should also express sympathy and regret, and thank the person for the loyalty and work they've put into the organization.

Redundancy hurts, so it's no surprise that many people who are made redundant will seek redress, possibly through an industrial tribunal. They are less likely to do this if they can see you have been fair, and if you make them feel appreciated despite the redundancy. If they take you to an industrial tribunal despite this, at least be sure you can justify your actions.

One of your top people is threatening to leave

If you really want to keep your employee, you will have to do something to persuade them to stay. So what can you do? Well, if they're threatening to go, they must be unhappy with things as they are. So, if they haven't already told you, ask them what it is they want. It could be any number of things, such as:

- more money
- more responsibility
- promotion
- better working conditions or hours

. . . or something else. If you don't ask them, you won't know.

Now ask yourself a very simple question. Are they worth what they're asking for? If they are, give it to them (you may be able to negotiate them down a bit – they're probably expecting that). If they're not worth it, let them go.

Aha, but what if you *can't* give them what they want? Most people aren't stupid – they can see what is and isn't possible. If budgets are tight, they can see a rise is out of the question. If there's nowhere to go, of course a promotion is difficult (although see 'You've got nowhere to promote a star performer but you don't want to lose them', page 9). A smart employee should be able to come up with creative solutions; it's in their own interest. They may suggest a performance-related pay component, or a better job title or a company car.

People don't threaten to leave unless they believe you can give them what they want to make them stay. If the only thing that will do is a pay rise or a promotion that clearly isn't feasible, they won't threaten. The first you'll know about it is when they hand in their notice.

There are a couple more pointers to bear in mind. First, don't allow yourself to be held to ransom. Many people threaten to leave in a very reasonable and genuine way. You can see that it makes sense for them to go if they can't move up the career ladder where they are. But some people are playing games, making threats to call your bluff and see what they can squeeze out of you. If you feel you're being taken for a ride, you may be better off letting the person go. Otherwise they may take what you give them and then leave anyway – with a better salary and job title as leverage for negotiations with their next employer.

The most common trap bosses fall into is to promise the person what they want at some unspecified time in the future and then never follow through on the promise. They seem to think that if they ignore the problem it will go away. In fact, of course, it won't. Suppose you tell the person you'll promote them as soon as you can but six months later there's no sign of a promotion. If they've got any sense, they'll leave. So if someone tells you they can't stay unless you further their career in some concrete way, you should take that threat extremely seriously. If you don't want to lose them, take action fast.

You've got nowhere to promote a star performer

If you don't want to lose them, it is important to talk to this person and explain the problem. Let them know that you're well aware they are worthy of promotion, but no positions look likely to come up in the foreseeable future. You may then be able to come up with an alternative between you. The most effective solution is to create a new position for them. Top people often have a knack of recognizing gaps you may have missed yourself. They might well say, 'I've been thinking increasingly that we could really do with someone to be a liaison point for all the regional marketing departments,' or 'I've always wanted to set up and run an internal magazine, and I believe we need one here.'

You might devise an entirely new position, or a variation on the current one but with more responsibilities and a better job title. You may both need to go away and think about it, but there's a good chance you'll come up with something which will challenge your top performer *and* benefit the organization.

The alternatives to this are to offer your team member cosmetic changes to their job, such as an improved job title or a bigger office. These can work in the short term if you think a promotion opportunity is likely to come up in, say, six to twelve months. But star performers aren't stupid and they will see these as the hollow offers they ultimately are. What they really want is an interesting challenge, so you need to find them one if you want to keep them.

You can only promote one of several good candidates in your team

If you approach this exercise rationally and fairly the problem will not be who to promote, but how to do it without demoralizing the team both during the selection and after the promotion.

The first thing to do is to advertise the post internally and invite all the candidates to apply. This ensures that no one feels they have been overlooked, or that they weren't considered for the post when they wanted to be. It may seem to be inviting trouble, but in fact it will mean that everyone can see the process is fair.

It would generally be wise to advertise the position externally as well. The extra candidates dilute the sense of competition within the team, and whoever gets the job may well be greeted with relief simply for not being an outsider. (If you end up wanting to give the job to an outside applicant, see 'You have several candidates for promotion within your team but you want to give the job to an outsider', page 12.)

Now make sure the selection procedure is scrupulously fair, and open, so your team can all see how fair it is. Don't cut corners if all your applicants are internal, but treat the process as formally as you would any selection procedure. Don't shortlist, unless all your internal applicants are on the shortlist. It drags out the process, and those who fail to make the shortlist will feel dreadful.

Once you have informed the successful applicant that they've got the job, call all the others in individually and let them know they've been unsuccessful.

Don't tell them individually who has got it. (See also 'One of your team is very disgruntled at being passed over for promotion' page 14.)

Once they've had half a day or so to digest this, call the whole team together – including those who weren't applicants for the post – and announce the promotion (they'll probably all know by now anyway, but that's not the point). Say how strong the candidates were, and how much you appreciated the amount of interest in the job. Then say that you realize it's been a difficult situation but you're sure you can count on everyone to support the successful candidate.

Once the person takes up their new post, keep a watchful eye to make sure everyone else is working comfortably alongside them. If there are any teething problems, talk to the person concerned and help to iron out any problems they're having.

"Don't cut corners if all your applicants are internal, but treat the process as formally as you would any selection procedure."

You have several internal candidates for promotion but you want to give the job to an outsider

Obviously you must give the job to the best applicant, whoever they are. There's no point inviting outside applications if you aren't seriously going to consider them (as well as this being unfair on the applicants). So if your best candidate is an outsider, don't be put off giving them the job by your fears about the team's reaction.

Make sure, however, that every member of the team has the opportunity to apply for the job on equal terms with each other and all the outside applicants. That way at least they won't feel they've been forgotten or not given a chance to put their case across.

> "If your best candidate is an outsider, don't be put off giving them the job by your fears about the team's reaction".

When you've made your decision, talk to each internal applicant in turn, telling them face-to-face that they haven't been successful this time. Don't be drawn on the question of who has got the job. (See also 'One of your team is very disgruntled at being passed over for promotion' page 14.) Thank them for their application and let them know you'll be happy to discuss how they can develop their skills with an eye to future promotion.

Call the whole team together, including those who didn't apply for the promotion, and tell them who has got the job. Make it clear that you were determined to be fair, and this person turned out to be the most suitable for the job. Remember to state that the standard of applications was very high, and you appreciate everyone's hard work.

Let the team know that you realize this is a potentially tricky situation. Remind them that the successful candidate is unaware that there were several internal applicants and that it is you, not they, who made the decision. So they deserve to be welcomed and supported when they arrive, and indicate that you trust the team not to make things difficult for them.

One of your team is disgruntled at being passed over for promotion

You can minimize this problem by breaking the news to the person the right way in the first place. Be extremely gentle with them; missing out on promotion is a huge blow to their ego as well as meaning that they don't get the challenge/pay rise/job title they were hoping for. Battered pride is a big part of what makes people upset at missing a promotion.

If you still have problems, call the person in for a meeting and talk to them about the reasons they missed out on the promotion. You should:

- be totally objective. Don't give any hint of bias towards the person who got the job, and make sure you can give fair and objective reasons for not promoting this particular person. Concentrate on the reasons they didn't get the job, rather than telling them how much better the other person was.

- explain what you were looking for in the applicants for the post. Tell the person what criteria you were judging by – level of experience, specific skills and qualifications, strengths and so on.

- ask the person to assess themselves against each of these criteria. Help by telling them, if they don't recognize it themselves, which criteria they failed to meet. If they disagree, you should be able to give them concrete examples of past performance which demonstrate that they didn't come up to standard.

- be positive about those criteria they did meet, now that you have made it clear why they failed to get the job. Build their confidence by letting them know where their work is up to standard.

- compensate them if you can by offering them a new contract to look after, or a new responsibility to take on, so they feel they still have your faith and they have a challenge to inspire them.

- talk to them about any future promotion prospects. Start working with them now, if they want to, on getting their performance up to scratch ready for the next promotion opportunity.

> "Battered pride is a big part of what makes people upset at missing a promotion."

Your team is trying really hard but there's no money for pay rises

If there's really no money, a pay rise isn't an option. However, that doesn't mean you can't reward your team. One of the functions of a pay rise is that it demonstrates that you recognize the person's hard work and achievements. For some, this recognition is even more important than the extra money. So you can go a long way to making up for the tight budget by finding other ways to reward good performance.

Call your team together and tell them that there's no money for pay rises. Make it very clear that you wish there were, and that they thoroughly deserve them, but it simply isn't possible right now. However, indicate that you have no intention of letting such good work go unrewarded, so you'll be looking for non-financial rewards instead. Invite them to come up with suggestions at their individual salary reviews – this gives them time to think about it.

There are all sorts of non-financial rewards you can give your team, and each member of it will probably have their own ideas about what will be important to them. You don't have to give them what they ask for – any more than you have to give them the pay rise they ask for – but obviously the closer you can get to what they want, the happier they will be. Here are a few ideas of the kind of things you might be able to offer them:

- commission/performance-related pay
- childcare contribution
- company car
- home computer

> "You can go a long way to making up for the tight budget by finding other ways to reward good performance".

- mobile phone
- health club membership
- more holiday allowance
- bigger office/office refurbishment
- flexi-time hours
- working from home one day a week
- more trips away from the office
- a promise of a pay rise at a later date, which will be higher than otherwise to compensate for its being late.

One of the advantages of this approach is that, since it is hard to put a value on most of these, it's hard to compare them. So you can give each team member the kind of reward they personally value.

You inherit a team of people who are hostile to you

This can happen for all sorts of reasons. Assuming your management style is not to blame (see 'Your team complain that they don't like your management style', page 19), it's likely that the reason is out of your control. Perhaps you've come from a part of the organization they are naturally hostile to, or maybe they particularly wanted someone else in the job. Whatever the reason, how do you handle it?

The key is not to try to tackle the whole team at once, but to work on each individual within it. If you can win the trust of each team member individually, it won't be long before the collective attitude follows suit. You still need to be firm and clear in your management, so don't try to buy your way into your team's affection by giving them lots of perks or going too easy on them. These kind of tactics always backfire.

Adopt your natural style and be tough when you need to be. But try to spend time with each of your team members so they get to know you better. Use opportunities such as business trips, exhibitions and so on to take one or other of your team along too. If they are hostile because they see you in an impersonal light – 'the person who supplanted their choice of manager', or 'a mouthpiece for senior management' – they won't be able to maintain this impersonal attitude once you become a real person to them.

Your team don't like your management style

If one person on your team is unhappy about your style and the rest are satisfied with it, it shouldn't be cause for concern. Everyone has their own preferences. But if a significant proportion of your team are unhappy with your style, you need to address the problem.

Start be calling a team meeting and ask them to let you know what changes they would like to see in your style. Let them know that so long as they are polite and pleasant you will appreciate constructive comment. They are your team, and you need them to tell you how you can get the best performance from them.

Not every criticism will necessarily be fair. However, as a guideline, the following qualities should all be part of your management style:

- be likeable
- be fair
- be trustworthy
- be positive and encouraging
- be an open communicator
- be available (not 24 hours a day, but frequently)
- be supportive of team members who need help
- be generous with acknowledgement and praise when it is deserved
- be clear about the team's goals, both individually and collectively
- be organized about work processes, projects, deadlines and systems

- be prepared to stand up for the team outside the department and take responsibility for its actions
- develop individuals' talents
- allow people to solve problems and carry out tasks in their own way so long as they meet the objective.

It is perfectly reasonable for any team to ask these basics of their manager. If your team feel you are not fulfilling any of these criteria, you should be honest and courageous enough to accept the criticism and work to change your management style.

> "Let them know that so long as they are polite and pleasant you will appreciate constructive comment."

The team is very hostile to senior management

This is normally triggered by some unpopular move or decision, but it can be very destructive in the long run. One of the team leader's hardest jobs is to inspire team loyalty to the whole organization. Joining in the abuse of top management is an easy cop out. You can't survive as a good team in a lousy company – you need the whole organization to succeed or you and your team members are all looking for a job. But if the management decision is a bad one, you can't pretend to your team that it's good. So what do you do?

- agree that it's bad
- remind your team of the wider considerations that the Board or management have to weigh up
- point out to them the weak points in the decision that they wanted
- compare your top managment to your competitors', pointing out how much better your own are.

Your team has to work with outsiders

Outside consultants, or auditors, drafted into the team can sometimes create a problem. The team may be suspicious, and want to know why – in the case of consultants – they weren't considered good enough to do the job themselves. You need to make sure that the relationship with the outsiders is an easy one, and doesn't damage morale. There are some steps you can take to help ease the situation.

- Tell the team in advance when outsiders are coming in, and why. Explain to the team how the outsiders will help them to meet their objectives.

- People will often not say when they feel ousted, so put their minds at rest without waiting for them to express their worries. Explain that the consultant was brought in for example, because the task was specialized (this may be obvious to the team), because you needed someone objective (perhaps for appearances' sake, so that's no reflection on the objectivity of your team members) or because you couldn't spare any of the team members because their own work was too important.

- Treat outsiders in the same way as the team while they're around. If you're taking the team down to the pub for a lunchtime drink, invite them along too. This will help to integrate them with the team.

You have to guide your team through major changes

The sort of big change that makes your job tough could be caused by mergers and takeovers, restructuring, new legislation that affects the team's working practices, relocation and so on. Some people love change, and revel in the challenge of it. You have to make sure that these team members don't either belittle or leave behind the people who are more resistant to change.

To start with, warn the team of impending changes as far in advance as possible, and fill them in on all the details you can. Regardless of your private views, give a positive view of the changes and explain how they will benefit the organization, the department and your team members.

Involve them in any decisions you can by holding team meetings and inviting comments, questions and suggestions. Encourage people to express any negative feelings and listen sympathetically – they may resist change because it threatens their security, because they know they are slow learners or because they think it will make their role less important or their job less stimulating. Ask them to be very specific about their objections then deal with each one individually. There will naturally be some genuine disadvantages resulting from the changes; admit to these but explain how they are more than offset by the benefits.

When the changes have been made, make regular checks with the resistors to see how they are adapting. Keep doing this until they tell you they are settled.

Your team is badly overstretched

Teams can be overstretched because of unreasonable demands from senior management or because of long term absence by someone in the team – perhaps because of illness, for a sabbatical, or on maternity leave. Recognition of the problem is vital here. Acknowledge that your team members are under pressure and give them plenty of thanks and rewards. There are things that you can do to help them.

- Be available. Yes, this is always important but especially so here. It's not just that people are working harder, but they may be doing jobs they are unfamiliar with or at speeds they are unused to. So they may well need more understanding, need to ask a lot of questions or want help with prioritizing their workload.

- Be prepared to lower your standards. Again, if people are trying to do more work in the same length of time, something may well have to give. Accept that not everything can always reach the same standard it does when the team is relatively relaxed.

- Share the extra workload. If someone is away, say on maternity leave, and you are sharing their tasks between the rest of the team, take some of them on yourself. Or you could free someone else up to do extra by relieving them of one of their regular tasks – but make sure it is not their favourite one, or one that means a lot to them for status reasons or whatever. To be safe, say to them, 'I could probably take over some of your work for a while so you're free to look after Angela's customers as well as your own. Is there anything you'd like to pass on to me?'

- Do something about the workload if you possibly can. Sometimes the pressure lasts for a predetermined length of time. But sometimes it can go on indefinitely. Eventually your words of sympathy and understanding will begin to sound hollow, and the team will start to feel that as long as you keep telling them they're wonderful, you think that excuses you from ever having to do anything about the problem.

> "Acknowledge that your team members are under pressure and give them plenty of thanks and rewards. There are things that you can do to help them."

Your team is split over a controversial policy issue

You have a big problem if there is such strong disagreement in the team about the collective goal that it splits the group. For example, if the team can't agree whether it should concentrate on the domestic or industrial market. You need to identify the problem as early as you can. In many cases this is just a matter of not ignoring it in the hope it will go away. The sooner you take action the better – and if you can pre-empt a split completely that's even better. You can't act too soon.

Call a team meeting and discuss the issues. The aim of the meeting is to reclarify the team's objectives. If you have built a strong team, its members will want to reach agreement and they will understand the importance of doing so. Your job is to make sure that this happens. Once a decision has been made, you need to make it evident that it is final. There's no point in your team members continuing to discuss the merits and demerits of the various options because it's too late. So whatever you do, don't let them think it's open for review later.

It can help to follow up the session with an increased workload (within reason) or a major challenge to the team. You can often create this by bringing forward a project the team would normally have started work on in a few weeks time. The object of the exercise is to unite the team in a common cause, and put them under just enough pressure that they don't have time to dwell on past decisions and emotions but focus on future plans.

One of the best ways to unite the team is to focus them on threats, dangers, rivals or enemies outside the team. If you can make them feel that survival is at stake and the enemy is beating at the gates, internal disputes will seem less important. It is on the same principal (if a little more dramatic) that dictators often start foreign wars to forestall revolution at home. Get the team involved in countering a competitor's new customer service campaign, for example, or coming up with solutions to the problems posed by new restrictive legislation.

"The sooner you take action the better – and if you can pre-empt a split completely that's even better. You can't act too soon."

There's a status battle within your team

This can be tough to deal with as the result is that the team fractures into factions that form around two key players on the team who have different aims for the team, different styles of working or different ambitions for themselves.

This situation can only arise if the two people involved are pulling in different directions in some way. You need to refocus them on the team: its needs and its objectives. Begin by calling the two people together and mediate while they discuss their differences, following the guidelines for feedback on page 146.

The greatest danger in these situations will come if you are weak in the way you handle them. You will need to be firm with these two, and tell them that the split in the team could not be happening unless they are allowing it to. Point out that the team is suffering as a result of the split, and that if they are committed to the team they must smooth out their differences and work to reunite the team.

The most important question to address these people with is, 'What is the best way for the team to accomplish the task?' Once you retreat to, 'What is the best way to keep A happy, or stop B sulking?' you are on a very slippery slope. People will realize that success depends on the force of their personalities not the force of their arguments.

If the situation has reached a critical point, or the people involved are not willing to co-operate, it may well be necessary to point out that if they do not have the necessary commitment to the team there is no place for them in it.

There is a personality clash within your team

You may have two strong personalities in your team that don't see eye to eye. This will cause problems for the whole team. You have to address the two people involved face on by sitting down with them and talking through the problem. You have to get them together, otherwise they will each wonder what you said to the other, and they may even misrepresent you to each other. This could make the problem worse rather than better, and it could even turn into a three way conflict that you have unintentionally become entangled in. When setting up this meeting make sure you:

- create a relaxed, informal setting in which to discuss the problem, at a time when no one is under time pressure.

- make it clear from the start that your job is to focus on objectives and to ensure that the team works towards them as effectively as possible. Their conflict is inhibiting that process, and you want to resolve it for the sake of the team. Explain that you do not wish to allocate blame, you simply want to resolve the problem.

- ask them to accept you as a mediator. Tell them that you believe that talking through the problem will resolve it, but get their agreement that if there are any points they cannot resolve they will accept your decision on them. These can always be reviewed later if the difficulties persist.

- set guidelines for the discussion, such as each allowing the other to finish what they are saying, focusing on the problem and not each other's personality, talking about their own feelings and reactions rather than focusing on the other person's actions.

- keep out of the discussion as much as possible, only stepping in to remind them of the guidelines if they start to stray from them.

- make absolutely sure that you give no indication whatsoever of any personal bias. If you think one of them is being more unreasonable or difficult than the other, don't let either of them see it. You are a referee only, so don't express an opinion.

- don't allow them to finish the meeting without an agreement – a verbal contract – about their future behaviour. If one person is in any way coerced into this arrangement they are unlikely to follow it, so you need to make sure that it is a genuinely mutual agreement. Make sure that one of them isn't making all the concessions in order to keep things sweet, but that they are both taking steps to meet each other halfway.

- do anything you can to help in your capacity as team leader. For example they may ask you to reallocate certain tasks, reprioritize them or to rearrange the office layout so the two work physically closer together or further apart. You brought these two people together to resolve their differences, so it's important that you are seen to co-operate when it comes to taking practical steps to achieve that resolution.

- arrange a date to review things after a few days or weeks (whichever seems appropriate). This way no one feels they have to commit themselves to an arrangement they might not be happy with when they try it, and if it only partly solves the problem they have a chance later to discuss further action.

- thank both of them for co-operating in trying to resolve the problem at the end of the meeting. At the review session, you should thank them again for any success they have had in making their solution work. Tell them you recognize that it isn't always easy, and that by managing to improve matters they have benefited the team as a whole.

You have to chair a meeting where emotions are running high

Disagreements can be a healthy way to force new ideas out, and often lead to even better solutions. Trouble is, people can become emotionally involved, and rational disagreement quickly changes to aggressive argument.

There is a four stage process for bringing overheated discussions back off the boil, and keeping the meeting moving forward in the process:

1. let people let off steam

2. be neutral

3. involve the rest of the group

4. keep to the facts.

The sooner you bring these techniques into play when you see trouble brewing, the less heated things will get.

"It is much easier to keep the peace than to regain it once it has been lost. So as soon as the mood starts to heat up, take action".

Let people let off steam

The first principle is that once strong feelings are aroused, it is counterproductive to attempt to repress them. You know yourself that if you are angry and someone tells you to calm down, it just makes you want to clout them. And the thing that irritates most of all is the feeling that no one is listening. So as soon as you sense heated emotions, ask the person concerned to express them. This opportunity to let off steam will help them feel that the group is at least listening to them, and will enable them to calm down by themselves. Ask what's wrong and insist that the rest of the team listens without interrupting for a few moments, until the person has got their feelings out in the open.

Of course, you don't want a fight to develop. If you feel this is a danger, come down firmly on any remarks that are getting personal and don't allow bickering or arguing to start. You can intervene and let each person have their say in turn, but get them to speak through you rather than directly to each other until tempers begin to cool down.

Once people have had their say and got their aggression out of their system, they tend to calm down by themselves. When angry they will often be pigheaded, but once they are calmer it is easier to get them to listen to rational argument, and to express their own point of view more reasonably.

Be neutral

It is essential that you are seen to be on no one's side but, rather, on the group's as a whole. Your focus is on resolving the debate amicably and sensibly, without wasting time on it. So whatever you do:

- avoid getting drawn into the argument
- don't start allocating blame

- don't criticize anyone for having strong feelings: they are entitled to them so long as they express them without getting personal

- don't lose your cool, or you will also lose credibility and respect.

There are times when someone's behaviour at a meeting really is out of line. No matter what the provocation, it isn't on to threaten violence, or to be deeply personal. But if one of your team deserves to be pulled up for this kind of behaviour, do it later and in private. Giving them a dressing down in front of the meeting will only increase their anger, as well as show you up to be thoroughly unprofessional.

Involve the rest of the group

When two angry people lock horns they often lose sight of what is going on around them. One of the best techniques for diluting their emotions is simply to bring other people into the debate. Of course, if you ask other people just to add their opinions to the argument you are simply encouraging it to expand and drag in the rest of the team. The trick is to change the subject subtly. Keep to the same topic, but ask someone else for a new angle on it. Look for something that will move the discussion on. You want to add new facts, bring in a new perspective or shed light on the cause of the problem

Suppose the argument is about whether the new brochures should be delayed to incorporate the new autumn product range, or whether they should be ready in time for the May mailshot. You could bring in someone else by asking the following sorts of questions.

'Ellen, you've been involved in this for four or five years now. What has happened in the past?'

'Tom, would it be possible to get the brochure out by May?'

'How about giving the new products their own supplementary brochure, Hilary? That's what you used to do at your last company isn't it?'

The aim here is not to shut out the warring parties, but simply to calm them down. Even angry people can have a valid point to make, and they may well be right. So don't exclude their point of view; just give them some time to relax and calm down while others are speaking.

Keep to the facts

This is another useful way to keep tempers from flaring. If people express their opinions they are bound to take sides in some way, whether they want to or not. So avoid opinions, rather stick to facts. They are much harder to argue with. Ask questions such as, 'What have we done about this in the past?' or 'How much more would two brochures cost?' If anyone tries to respond with an opinion, simply say, 'Let's stick to facts for the moment . . .' and then repeat the question.

Ideally, you should be able to spot trouble brewing and stop it before it starts. It is much easier to keep the peace than to regain it once it has been lost. So as soon as the mood starts to heat up, take action. Respond to the first personal snipe you hear with something like, 'Let's not get personal. We're not discussing what went wrong last time. We need to decide what lead times we need on this contract.'

Rumours and gossip are damaging morale and performance

The way to prevent gossip and rumour that damage your team is to be open and honest with them and to communicate clearly and fully. Secrecy is the breeding ground of rumour. Once your team know that if something were true you would have told them about it, they will be far less inclined to believe dangerous gossip.

Make sure your team understands that if they hear gossip that affects their work they should come straight to you and simply ask you if it's true. When they discover that you're always happy to talk through this sort of thing with them, and that you'll tell them anything you can, they won't need to spread gossip in future.

Of course, the occasional rumour will slip past the system. When this happens, you need to call in the person you believe is initiating or spreading it. If you're not sure, take a guess – it won't matter that much. But remember, you're only concerned about work-related rumours. If your team wants to whisper about the fact that John on reception's marriage is breaking up, that's none of your business. Once you have the person in your office make sure you:

- aren't tough on them – treat it as though this could be useful information rather than mere rumour. After all, until you've discussed it with them you don't know – maybe it is true. For example, say to them, 'I understand that you've been passing on the news that the sales department may be relocating to the Midlands. What can you tell me about it?' Ask them to give you the details, where they heard it from, the evidence behind the information and so on.

- telephone the relevant people to confirm the story. Call the sales manager, for example, and ask whether the team is moving. If the person with you did not initiate the rumour themselves, don't give them a hard time – they'll be feeling embarrassed enough as it is. And by the time you've finished talking to them you may well have rooted out the real culprit.

Once your team discovers that this is how you react to gossip they will think again before they spread rumours in future; no one wants to go through that kind of embarrassment.

You have to keep the team happy through an office move

Office moves are something that most team leaders find incredibly frustrating. A good team will handle the practical side of the move with little difficulty; the disruptive nature of the process is caused by status issues rather than operational ones.

This is because some desks or offices are considered more 'important' than others. But the argument never admits this – it's always conducted in operational terms: 'I need to be near the car park to carry in boxes of samples' or 'How can I conduct selection interviews in an open plan office?' It's rarely any use bringing the status subtext out into the open; people always deny it. But if you are aware of it you can often adjust some other status factor upwards for example, by putting the person's name on the door, or giving them their own business card, a change of job title from 'operator' to 'executive' or something else that will placate them.

Take into account the fact that status doesn't float in mid-air: it is relative to the people around. So it may be that the only reason John isn't happy with the office you allocated him is because he doesn't think it's as good as the one you allocated Pat, and he sees his role as being equally important to Pat's. In this case, you can use the same approach, but if you give Pat as well as John business cards or a new job title you won't have achieved anything. Try to give these kind of rivals completely different status symbols from each other so it becomes hard for them to compare themselves. Which is better, a plusher office or a better-sounding job title? Hard to say really – and hopefully John and Pat will find it pretty hard to say too.

There's a crisis and you have to manage the team through it

Most managers adopt the same attitude to handling a crisis – they trust themselves to make the right decisions when it comes to thinking on their feet. To some extent this is unavoidable because you simply don't know what the emergency is going to be. It could be the building catching fire, a customer collapsing in reception, a bomb scare or something you have never even thought of, such as squirrels in the roof eating through the electric cables, perhaps, or a gang of terrorists holding the team hostage. Nevertheless there are certain precautions you can take that will stand you in good stead in most crises of this kind:

- Make sure that your team has at least one qualified first aider. Don't simply ask for volunteers, though. Draw up a list of people in the team who are usually on the premises, and then cross off the names of all the ones whom you suspect would be likely to go to pieces in an emergency. You now have a list of viable first aiders. Decide who would be the best in a crisis and ask them if they would be happy to be trained. You can't push people into something like this so if they prefer not to, simply move on to the next person on the list and ask them. If groups within the team are often elsewhere – for example if they attend a lot of trade shows with heavy display stands or potentially dangerous demonstration equipment to set up – you may decide that one of them should also take first aid training. After the course, it can be very helpful to ask the new first aider to talk to the team meeting about the main things they got out of the course.

- Take their training seriously. I can tell you from personal experience that if you send someone on a one day first aid course and never mention the fact again then, five years on, if faced with someone who has stopped breathing or is bleeding profusely, they won't have a clue what they're supposed to do. First aid training has to be topped up regularly.

- Work out what the broad general categories of emergencies are and talk them through with your team. Plan what you would do if they ever happened. This kind of planning session could be crucial if you ever come up against one of these situations – and you probably will sooner or later – but the planning will also help bring the team closer together. You haven't got time to discuss every eventuality but discuss, say, what you'd do in the event of a fire and what you'd do if someone collapsed and an ambulance had to be called. There may be other potentially dangerous situations that are peculiar to your business, such as a chemicals leak or sensitive electronic equipment in the basement being flooded out.

- Some crises are over in an instant and only take one or two clear headed people to deal with them. But some last longer – perhaps you need to ask for volunteers to stay late or work over the weekend cleaning up your flooded basement and rescuing your sensitive electronic equipment. In these cases it's important to involve everyone, or the ones you leave out will feel they're not wanted. So find ways to make everyone feel they helped save the day.

- The people who helped you get through the crisis want and deserve your appreciation. It's probably about the only reason they worked their socks off in the first place. So don't be coy about it. Tell them how wonderful they are. And to show you're not just being glib, tell them exactly why: 'I don't know how you kept all those customers calm,' or 'Where did you learn so much about electrics? We'd have been lost without that'. Don't just tell your team how great they were. Tell everyone else too. Send a special report praising them to the board of directors, write an article for the corporate newsletter or put them forward for a corporate award. And give them a thank you present. If they worked together to get the computer back up, take them all out for a slap up meal. If they saved half a dozen lives, buy them a car. Match the reward to the action. But make sure you reward them.

One of the plus points of managing a crisis is that the situation tends to encourage teamwork. Everyone pulls together as a Blitz mentality takes hold. The only bar to this is poor communication. Get your communication with the team right, and you should get through the crisis smoothly. Here are the seven key rules to ensure you never inadvertently make a drama out of a crisis:

1. keep everyone in the team informed of what's going on all the time

2. assemble the team en masse to give them important information or directions

3. encourage them to ask questions if they want more information or don't understand anything

4. involve them in all key decisions; give them as much control as possible

5. be available in case any of them wants to come and discuss the problem with you. That means not only being there physically, but also listening properly to what they have to say

6. let them see that you're on their side: putting their case to other departments, senior management or whoever, finding out what resources they need to cope with the problem and doing your best to provide them

> "Laughter is the best way
> in the world to
> reduce stress".

7. never lose your sense of humour. Laughter is the best way in the world to reduce stress. And if you join in or even initiate the humour the rest of the team will see you as being more cool and in control than they otherwise might. It takes the pressure off them because it indicates that you're not about to bawl them out for the slightest mistake.

You have to deal with a system failure

The computer has crashed, the switchboard's gone down or the exhibition displays have been stolen the night before the biggest trade show of the year. What on earth do you do? These problems often give you some time to think, and even plan. All right, by normal standards it may not seem like it but, compared to a customer collapsing on the premises with heart failure, this sort of crisis is a luxury. So make the most of it. Resist the temptation to rush blindly into the thick of things as soon as trouble strikes, and hold an emergency planning session with your team instead, in which you:

- **define the problem.** The problem is not that the switchboard has gone down, it is that no one can get through on the telephone and you can't make calls out. That means no telephone orders, no complaints, no customer enquiries, no contact with suppliers, no cold calls and so on. It shouldn't take a moment to do this, but it makes a difference if you know that the objective is not to mend the switchboard but to restore communication with customers and suppliers. This may seem like a waste of time, but it's not. If you define the problem clearly like this, it makes it far easier to find alternative solutions. Instead of everyone's mind being fixed on switchboards, they are far more likely to think of temporary solutions such as drafting in mobile phones or visiting key customers by car.

- **prioritize the different parts of the problem.** Which of these matters most? Incoming calls from customers? Contact with suppliers? You may be able to find the resources for a temporary solution to part of the problem. You need to know which part to channel them into. For example, suppose the switchboard has failed in such a way that the switchboard handset works

42   HOW TO HANDLE TOUGH SITUATIONS AT WORK

fine for incoming and outgoing calls, but it won't route anything through to the extensions. This effectively leaves one telephone to share between everyone. If you have decided that the top priority is to contact certain key suppliers for emergency orders, and the next priority is for customers to get through, your problem is solved. Use the phone to make your outgoing crucial calls to suppliers first, and then use it only for incoming calls.

- **brainstorm the options.** Say your exhibition stand has been stolen at the last minute. You could cancel your appearance at the show, you could appear without a stand, you could agree a budget and try to cobble together a stand over the next six hours or you could call your branch 200 miles away and ask them to courier *their* exhibition stand to you. Everyone should be free to contribute to this brainstorming session (which only needs to take two or three minutes if that's all you've got).

- **take *only* the decisions you need to.** Don't say 'We'll hold all the orders at the moment to put on the computer when it's up and running again; if it's not fixed by midday we'll start processing them manually.' You don't know what will be happening by midday. Maybe you'll know by then that the computer will be working again by half past, maybe only one order will have come in all morning or maybe 500 will have come in by 10 a.m.. Don't make advance decisions – you haven't got time. Concentrate on the decisions that can't wait. Just say 'We'll hold all the orders for the moment' and leave it at that. Then review the situation every so often.

- **allocate tasks.** You've defined the problem, prioritized the most important parts of it to address, established the options and made the decisions that needed to be made straight away. This has probably taken between three and ten minutes. Now you need to allocate tasks so everyone in the team knows what they're doing, and there's no inadvertent doubling up.

- **make sure everyone understands clearly.** You're not the only one who's under pressure, and this is where miscommunication can lead to catastrophe. Stay calm and invest an extra minute or two in making sure that everyone knows exactly what they should be doing.

Your team is demoralized after a failure

Sometimes bad news isn't simply a matter of poor luck. Perhaps the team has lost a contract they've been working for months to win, for the simple reason that it wasn't as good as their competitor's. Or perhaps your team's negligence caused four deaths when a car crashed through a safety barrier that should have stopped it – your team built the crash barrier and never noticed the fault. All the guidelines for breaking bad news apply (page 50), along with a few more.

First, don't try to cover up failure; admit it. Then make it clear that *you* are not displeased with *them* – because you're one of them; you may all be dissatisfied with yourselves collectively. Let them see that you recognize that as team leader you carry the greatest responsibility.

Your job, in relation to your own superiors, is to take the blame yourself but to give credit to your team and its members when it is due (as the old army maxim says: there are no bad soldiers, only bad officers). Your team members need to know that you are in it with them, and that you aren't putting the blame on them when you talk to people outside the team.

Hold a session with your team to analyze the mistakes or weaknesses. Point out to them that if you can learn from your mistakes you should be better

> "First, don't try to cover up failure; admit it".

than anyone next time – you'll be the last people to make *that* mistake again. But it's crucial to identify and accept your failings.

Remind your team that nothing is all bad. There must have been some things that you all did well and you need to know what they were so you don't reject them along with the mistakes. This gives you a strong positive note to end the session on.

Once a day or so has gone by, start to joke about the mistake. You might as well – you've got nothing to lose. It keeps the atmosphere light and shows your team that it may not be good to fail, but it's not the end of the world. It will ease the pressure on everyone. There are some points to bear in mind, however:

- be wary of joking about a failure that has led to serious illness, injury or death

- don't direct jokes against any member of the team (except yourself, if you wish)

- don't make jokes that reinforce the team's sense of inadequacy. Every joke has a butt, so try to focus yours on things like the competitor that won the contract, the specification for it, any minor mistake that was caused by the whole team and not just one member, minor details that were out of the team's control or anything else you can think of.

The team is demoralized because business is bad

There's not much you can do about the cause here, so you need to find ways to keep the team motivated despite the downturn.

- Adjust targets if necessary. If the team are working to targets that were set when things weren't looking so bad, those targets may now be unattainable. This is very demotivating. If you adjust the targets so they are more realistic, at least the team will still have the satisfaction of meeting them.

- Hold regular team meetings and keep everyone informed about the business climate generally as well as team matters. This will also help to cement the group as a team, which gives them an important emotional and mental boost.

- Work hard to inject some fun into work. It's no replacement for real job satisfaction in the long term, but it will help boost morale in the short term. Whether it's friendly competitions, office outings, sticky buns at coffee time or frisbee games during the lunch hour, help the team to enjoy the time they spend at work.

- Find a project the team can work on successfully. This may be an aspect of work that is still going well, or it may be a presentation or even an internal event such as an office party. The important thing is to find something that is challenging and will give the team a real feeling of success and satisfaction.

You have to give bad news to the team

Perhaps you've just heard you won't be moving to the smart new offices after all – your team is one of those staying in the grotty old building. Or maybe you've been through the budget and there's just no way you can find the money to take on a temp for three months to help get a key project finished on time; the team members are going to have to carry all the extra workload themselves. Or perhaps the board has just announced that it is planning redundancies, which will probably affect your team.

Some bad news affects the whole team and it's not a pleasant task having to break it to them. Their morale is likely to be seriously damaged and it can take a while to rebuild. So you need to be as positive as possible when you tell them the bad news – within reason: unbounded cheerfulness and optimism would be out of place.

- Tell them the reasons why the decision has been made. If you didn't make it yourself, find out the reasons from whoever did.

- Remind them of the team's objectives and reassure them that these can still be met, which is the top priority. If for any reason they *can't* be met because of this decision, agree fresh objectives in the light of the bad news, and reassure the team that they can meet these.

- Let them know that you are sorry they missed out, and that you feel they deserved to move into better offices or to have extra help on the project. However, obviously the wider picture didn't allow this to happen.

- Sometimes compensation is an option. For example, if they can't move offices perhaps you can arrange to refurbish the present ones. Or if you

> "Try to give them another challenge to put their energies into, preferably something you are pretty confident will work out well".

can't afford a temp for three months perhaps you *can* afford to contract out at least some of the work.

- Try to give them another challenge to put their energies into, preferably something you are pretty confident will work out well. For example, if your team has a real talent for organizing and giving presentations, try to arrange a key presentation sooner rather than later after bad news, to help distract them.

You have to break bad news to an individual team member

Perhaps one of your team members hasn't got the promotion they applied for, or their proposal to the board of directors has been turned down. The tough part of bad news interviews isn't imparting the news, but coping with the person's reaction to it. The most likely responses are silence, tears and other emotions or anger.

The silent response

You might argue that if someone doesn't want to talk, you shouldn't make them. That's fine if they really don't want to, but people often clam up because they're afraid to show their emotions or because they are – literally – speechless. To some extent you have to judge this for yourself, but it helps to take into account the person's normal character. If they are usually open and chatty, it's a bad sign if they won't speak. If they are generally quiet and relatively unemotional, perhaps they genuinely don't feel there's much to be said. There are certain things to bear in mind when dealing with this sort of response.

- Don't judge the gravity of the news on their behalf. You may think it's a minor setback, but to them it could be a catastrophe. If this is the case and you say, 'Don't worry, it's not the end of the world,' they will fear that if they show their feelings you'll think they're overreacting.

- Show them that their feelings are important. Make it clear that you've set aside plenty of time for this interview, and that you're concerned about how they cope with the news.

- Ask them questions – open questions – to get them talking. And encourage them to ask you questions. Don't say 'Have you got any questions?' because they'll probably say 'No'. Instead say 'What questions would you like to ask?'

- Arrange a time to talk again in a day or two, once they've had time to think. This will give them a chance to get over their initial shock or upset, without depriving them of the chance to ask questions or discuss the ramifications of the news.

- Never discuss what has been said in confidence at the interview with anyone else in the organization.

The emotional response

It's not unusual, when you give someone news they don't want to hear, for them to burst into tears. If you're not ready for it, it can be hard to handle. So when you call a bad news interview, always be prepared for the possibility that your team member may get emotional.

- Some people derive great comfort from a hug, or simply having someone hold their hand, when they're upset. You may find this easier to judge if you think about it in advance. Obviously it shouldn't be a rehearsed action, but a bit of forethought should tell you whether this person is normally tactile or physically distant from their friends and colleagues, and whether the nature of the news is likely to influence their feelings towards you. If the main reason they missed out on the promotion was because you recommended against it, you might be the last person they want anywhere near them. Take into account your respective sexes as well.

- Depending on your relationship with the person, and the nature of the news, you might want to have a third person present at the interview to comfort them if they need it. Since the interview is confidential you will have to choose someone appropriate, such as a representative of the personnel department. Or you could start the interview with just the two of you, but if they become emotional offer to call in a colleague they are close to (if they want you to do this, call the colleague on the internal phone for the sake of privacy).

- If they seem embarrassed about crying or showing their emotions in front of you, ask them if they'd like a few minutes on their own. Go and make them a cup of coffee, or make a quick phone call, so they can have five minutes to calm down. Equally, at the end of the interview let them stay put until they are ready to face their colleagues again. For this reason it's a good idea to hold bad news interviews somewhere away from your office, where you won't be disturbed.

- Don't give up on the interview. Some people may burst into tears in an attempt – conscious or unconscious – to persuade you to change your mind or do something more to prevent the situation. Most do it simply because they are deeply upset. Either way, you should be sensitive but don't be influenced by tears to change a decision you believe to be right. Quite apart from the need to follow the best course of action, your team would lose respect for you.

The angry response

If the bad news you are imparting involves a decision the person isn't going to like, they may be angry with you – whether it was your decision or one from higher up that you are simply passing on.

- People get angry because they feel they cannot get the response they want without getting angry. Usually they feel they are not being listened to. So the first thing to do is to listen to what they have to say. Hear them out, and they will begin to calm down.

- Show the person that you sympathize with their point of view. You may not be able to give them what they want, but you can still indicate that you appreciate their feelings. You can use phrases such as, 'I can see that must be frustrating for you', or 'No wonder you're feeling angry about it'.

- Don't wind them up by trying to justify your actions. It sounds as if you're making excuses, and are more interested in your side of the matter than in theirs.

- Let them see, kindly but firmly, that the decision won't be changed. They are entitled to feel angry, but they will be wasting their time if they try to use their anger to pressure you to change your mind.

- If you listen properly and sympathize without giving in, they will blow themselves out after a few minutes.

One of your team is suffering from work-related stress

Certain kinds of stress are perfectly healthy; you could call them 'positive stress'. Some people work better under pressure as it lends an excitement to work. If everything is easy, there are no challenges and no deadlines, things can get very boring. But there is also negative stress – too much pressure – which can be counterproductive, unhealthy and even dangerous. If one of your team is badly stressed you must do something about it as soon as you can.

Signs of stress

The first indications of a stressed team member are likely to be:

- taking work home regularly
- failing to take holidays.

If you don't tackle the problem, the next symptoms will include:

> "If one of your team is badly stressed you must do something about it as soon as you can".

- tiredness
- irritability
- criticizing other people
- carrying out tasks in a panicky or flappy manner
- poor concentration
- poor memory
- headaches or back pain.

Eventually, in the serious stages, the signs you should notice include:

- exhaustion
- apathy
- lack of commitment
- lack of enjoyment in their work
- a tendency to catch every bug going round
- sudden outbursts of emotion or shaking.

Identifying the causes

When someone on your team is stressed, you need to try to work out why. It helps if you can do this before you talk to them (it will only take you a few minutes to sit down and think it through), because it will be helpful to consider solutions that are in your power rather than theirs to apply, before you sit down and discuss it with them.

Here are the most common causes of stress at work; go through them and see which you think might apply to them:

- too many deadlines, or deadlines that are too tight
- frequent interruptions making it impossible for them to get anything done
- poor performance
- long hours
- workload too heavy
- poor prioritizing
- isolated working conditions
- bad working relationships
- insecurity/fear of redundancy.

These are the most common causes of work-related stress, but obviously the list is not complete. There may be conditions that are peculiar to your team that are contributing to stress among its members so you need to consider these as well.

You should find as you work through the list that you can narrow down the causes of stress in the team member you are concerned about, and may well be able to identify the solution quite easily.

Addressing the problem

Call the team member in for a meeting. Make sure you create a relaxed atmosphere and plenty of time to discuss the problem. Ask your team member to tell you what they think the cause is before you give them your opinion. If they are unsure, or you're not convinced that they have identified the full reason behind it, offer your opinion – note the word 'offer'. Don't say 'Let me tell you what I think . . .', say 'Do you think it's possible that it might be caused by . . .?'

Once you have agreed on the cause of the problem, you need to find a solution. And you must have the person's support for any solution or it may not work. The likelihood is that if you simply promise to remove the cause of the stress they'll feel instantly happier and their performance will improve along with their health. Unfortunately, though, there is a slight hitch with this. It's not always that easy to remove the cause of the stress. But it's generally possible to ameliorate it in some way. Here are the most common stress factors, and some solutions to them.

Deadlines

Have a look at their workload and see whether the deadlines are unreasonable. If they are, change the schedules or remove some of the workload. If you feel the deadlines are not unreasonable, talk them through with the person. You could set interim deadlines so they can never get too far behind: instead of saying 'I want this report on Friday week' say 'I'd like the outline for this report next Wednesday, and the first draft the following Tuesday. Then I'd like the finished document on Friday week.' It may also help to give the person some time management training.

Interruptions

Talk through the various methods of minimizing interruptions; they may not know the tricks of the trade. If they are underassertive they may find it hard to say 'not now' to people. Assertiveness or time management training may help. If their desk is open to the rest of the team, perhaps you could site them somewhere where they are less likely to be disturbed. Or allow them to use a meeting room or spare office for an hour or two when they're working on something that takes a lot of concentration.

Poor performance

If someone is stressed by this they clearly care, and will be doing their best to remedy it. It's likely, therefore, that they cannot help falling short of their targets. In this case see if you can identify the problem area (such as poor time management, for example, or too heavy a workload). Training may help, or it may be that you need to reduce their workload or adjust their targets to a more practical and achievable level.

Long hours

People who take work home are either trying to impress you or they have too much work. If they are trying to impress, let them know that they don't have to. Make it clear that you judge your team members' ability on what they can achieve during working hours. If they genuinely have too much work, do something about relieving the load.

Workload too heavy

Again, this could be poor time management, in which case training can help, or it may be that the workload really is too heavy, in which case you'll need to find ways to reduce it.

Poor prioritizing

Discuss the problems of prioritizing, and establish why they find it difficult. Give them training if necessary, and perhaps ask them to spend five minutes with you every Monday morning for the next few weeks to go through their priorities with you.

Isolated working conditions

Some people love to work alone, but for some it is a real stress provoker; they need human contact. Find a way for these people to spend more time around others, or perhaps take them out of a lone office and put them in an open-plan office.

Bad working relationships

If there is a persistent problem try to minimize contact between the people who don't get on – make sure they don't have to sit at neighbouring desks, for example. (See pages 29–30 for how to handle conflict within the team.)

Insecurity/fear of redundancy

Reassure your team member if you can. Occasionally, however, there is a real threat of redundancy or relocation. You can't change the facts, but the person's stress will be minimized if you keep them as fully informed as possible. Tell them what you can, and tell them when you'll know more. Keep them posted.

If you feel that someone is in an advanced state of stress you will need to suggest more drastic measures. You may even have to insist on certain things – kindly but firmly – for their own health. If you have a company counsellor or doctor you could refer them there. Otherwise try to persuade them to seek professional help themselves. If the symptoms are serious enough it may even be wise to suggest they take time off, or advise them strongly to take the holiday entitlement they haven't been using. Generally speaking, however, you should recognize the symptoms long before they reach this stage.

One of your team is going through a personal crisis

Severe personal problems can have a serious effect on someone's performance at work. Maybe they're ill, or having relationship problems or a member of their family has just died.

Some people question what their team members' personal problems have got to do with them. Wouldn't it be better to keep out of it altogether; surely it's none of their business? And some people consider it somehow soft – it doesn't matter what's going on in their team members' private lives, it's part of their staff's job to make sure it doesn't interfere with work.

It's true that, in a sense, your team members' private lives are none of your business, and certainly nothing, including poor performance at work, gives you the right to pry into details of it that your team member doesn't want to discuss. But very often they are more than happy to discuss the problem. They may not volunteer to talk about it because they're too proud, they think you're too busy, they're worried you'll think they can't cope or because *they* think it's not your problem and they've no right to dump it on you.

However, they'll have realized that it's spilling over into the workplace and affecting their performance or their behaviour, and they will be glad of the opportunity to talk round ways of solving the problem. It may be that they actually *can't* solve it without your help, because they need you to approve or authorize a particular course of action – such as leaving work an hour early for a couple of weeks until they've sorted out new childcare arrangements.

Dealing with the problem

So you know your team member has a personal problem. Maybe you know what it is, or maybe you're not certain. Either way, you're going to have to hold a counselling session with them. This is where a lot of managers, quite understandably, get a bit stuck. You probably got the job because of your abilities in organizing, setting objectives and targets, motivating people and a number of other related skills. And your training since has probably concentrated on developing those areas. Now suddenly you're supposed to be a professional counsellor as well.

Well, the good news is that counselling skills are a lot easier to learn than you might think. And the most important things are all about what *not* to do. So, as long as you avoid the worst mistakes, you can't go that far wrong.

The idea of counselling, in its simplest terms, is to talk to the person with the problem and arrive at a solution. That's all there is to it. But there are a few guidelines to go through to make sure that they are willing to talk, and to ensure that the end solution is one that will work. For a start, find a relaxed, private time to talk and make sure there are absolutely no interruptions. Then encourage your team member to talk about the problem by outlining the problem as you see it. For example, say, 'I've noticed that you've been arriving late at work/been much quieter than usual/been missing deadlines recently. Can you tell me the reason?' If you know for a fact what the problem is, you can be more direct but make it clear you're not prying. For example, 'You seem very pressured since your mother died, and your standard of work has suffered. Is there anything I can do to help?' Once your team member starts to talk, there are a few guidelines to follow, which are detailed below.

Acknowledge their feelings

Reassure them that their response to the situation is valid. Deep down, they're nervous you're going to say, 'Is that all? What on earth are you making a fuss about?' So reassure them with comments like, 'No wonder you're finding it difficult to cope' or 'That must be a real strain for you.' It often helps to boost people's self respect by saying something such as, 'I'm surprised you've been coping as well as you have'. Don't be insincere, but if you find something in their response to be complimentary about, say so.

One word of warning here: avoid telling anyone that you understand how they feel. You don't, and they know it. Some people may not mind – later on in the conversation they might even ask you to say it ('you do understand, don't you?') – but some people are upset and even angered by it. Of course you're only trying to help, but a significant number of people when told 'I understand' will respond by saying 'No you bloody don't!'

Encourage them to talk

Ask open questions (ones that start 'how', 'what' or 'why' and therefore beg full answers). The word 'why?', especially used on its own, can seem rather blunt, or even pushy. It can be better to ask 'What's the reason for that . . . ?' or 'What makes you think that?' It's also important to get the person to talk about their emotions; it's usually the emotions that cause the problems at work, after all. At this stage you are simply information-gathering – don't start volunteering your own comments. Just keep asking questions.

There's one other point about encouraging people to talk – don't judge. This will shut people up faster than anything. Whatever private opinion you may have, don't let them see it. No one likes being judged, and they won't put themselves in line for it; they'll just clam up. If it turns out that this team member's partner has just left them because they had a string of affairs, don't say: 'Well you've only yourself to blame really then, haven't you?' Remember your own objective – to help resolve their problem so that their performance will return to its previous level and the morale of the team won't be damaged. Passing judgement is not going to help you reach that objective.

Examine the options

Once you feel you have gathered all the relevant information you can, you need to guide the conversation onto the next stage. There isn't a fixed length of time a counselling session should take, but it will normally be between half an hour and an hour. If it goes on longer than this, it's probably become rambling and non-directional somewhere in the middle. So after about 15 to 30 minutes you should start to feel the time is right to move onto this stage.

This is not, repeat *not*, about giving advice. At this stage, the idea is to be totally neutral. You want to throw every option into the ring – and you want your team member to suggest as many of them as possible. It's their problem after all.

Start by saying something along the lines of, 'What do you think would help?' You can throw in the odd helpful comment, but don't attach any opinions to it. Don't indicate whether you think it's a good idea or a bad idea. It's just an option. For example: 'You could leave an hour earlier until the problem is sorted, in exchange for cutting your lunch break.' Then you're not expressing a view, you're simply stating a fact. You might privately think it would be better if your team member employed a nanny who could drive, or gave up their affair and persuaded their partner to return but it is not your place to say such things.

By the end of this stage of the counselling session you should have as broad a range of options as possible on the table. Most of the options that involve your team member's home situation will have been offered by them. You should, in particular, have offered options based on information that your team member may not have known, such as 'We have a staff counselling service here that I could refer you to'.

Find a solution

The key to finding a solution is to let the person with the problem find it. If they feel pressured into a solution they aren't happy with it's less likely to work. Not only that, but it's important to accept that they 'own' the problem. It's theirs. That means that it's their responsibility to find a solution to it – no one has the right to take it out of their hands. When someone is under stress and vulnerable they find it harder to say no, and it's far easier than you might think to pressure them unwittingly into adopting your preferred solution, if you let them find out what it is.

It should go without saying, therefore, that once they have decided which solution they are going to go for, you must agree to it without argument. You'll have discounted any non-options at the previous stage, such as 'I'm afraid we can't give you six months paid leave' so all the choices left are valid options. Support their solution and agree a course of action with them. For example, if they want to leave earlier for a few weeks, agree how many weeks they need the arrangement to stand for and set a date to review the situation shortly before this time limit expires.

Finally, as you conclude the counselling session, make it clear that if they want to talk again any time – about this problem, new developments or any other problem – your door is open.

Someone on your team is diagnosed HIV positive

Many people who are diagnosed HIV+ will choose to keep the fact private. But sometimes these things get out, or the person chooses to tell their colleagues. When this happens, the situation can call for careful handling.

Many team members will follow your lead. Make sure you continue to treat HIV+ sufferers in your usual way. Don't avoid touching them, but don't keep touching them to prove a point either. Don't patronize them by giving them special treatment, such as setting them lower standards or allowing them to turn up late in the mornings. If they develop AIDS they may ask for certain allowances to be made for their ill-health, but until this happens they don't need to be made a special case. The important thing is to let *them* tell you what they do and don't need. Otherwise, carry on as usual and expect your team to do the same.

If you have certain team members who are unhappy about working closely with someone who is HIV+, call them into your office and talk through their fears with them. Give them literature on the subject or suggest they talk to their doctor for reassurance. There are other steps that you may need to take:

- If the HIV+ team member is happy about it, you could hold an HIV-awareness session for the whole team. The person may be prepared to talk to the team themselves, or they may prefer you to arrange for an outside medical expert to present the session. Most fear of HIV and AIDS stems from ignorance, so the single most helpful thing you can do is to replace this ignorance with information.

- Once everyone knows the score, has talked through their fears until they are reassured and has been given all the information they want, make it a disciplinable offence to show prejudice towards the HIV+ team member.

> "Do not attempt to turn prejudiced people into unprejudiced people – simply ask them to *behave* like unprejudiced people while they're at work".

If you have fulfilled the previous criteria, it's unlikely to happen, but you must make it clear that you won't tolerate it. Be sensitive, however, towards the sufferer – they won't necessarily thank you if they become the cause of everyone else's verbal warnings. In the highly unlikely event that matters get out of hand, talk to this person first about the best way to handle the problem. You may not decide to do exactly what they ask, but you should listen and take their views into account.

- Unfortunately, prejudices are almost impossible to get rid of. Your best hope is to keep them hidden, and out of the way of the team's work. Do not attempt to turn prejudiced people into unprejudiced people – simply ask them to *behave* like unprejudiced people while they're at work.

Someone in the team is seriously ill or dies

This is about the most shocking thing that can happen in a team, and needs to be handled very delicately. Your team members will be at their most sensitive and will judge you harshly for any insensitivity you show. Having said that, don't be too nervous – they will see that you're shocked too and they will forgive you any mistakes made through being shell-shocked or inexperienced in dealing with such a situation. Here are some guidelines to help you:

- When you hear the news of death, accident or diagnosis of serious illness, call the whole team together and tell them all at once.

- Be prepared for some colleagues to be extremely upset; if you have a company counsellor or doctor, arrange to have them on hand. If the news is unexpected and shocking, give the person's close colleagues the rest of the day off – maybe longer. If you're not sure how long, err on the side of generosity. Never mind what happens about today's important meeting or presentation: if the team think you put work before people they will lose respect and loyalty towards you in a big way. And the strength of the team is more important than whatever is in the diary for today. Just about anybody will understand your cancelling an event or appointment, or shutting up shop for the day, because of serious accident or death.

- If the person has died, give their fellow team members time off to go to the funeral, and go to it yourself. Make sure the organization sends flowers, quite apart from anything that members of the team may do jointly or separately.

- Give the team plenty of time – maybe several weeks – to get back to normal (depending on the nature of the tragedy). Let them feel they can talk about it – don't allow it to become a taboo subject.

- If you make any mistakes, say so: 'I'm sorry I didn't give you all the day off on Friday. With hindsight I can see that we were all much more shaken than I realized at the time.'

- If one of your team members is diagnosed seriously ill but is still working, let them decide how to play it. They may want to keep it quiet or they may wish to tell people themselves, singly or as a team. Or they may want you to tell the team.

A top performer suddenly goes off form

When this happens, there has to be a reason. What's more, your top performer will realize they are delivering below their usual standard, and will probably be glad of the chance to discuss the problem with you.

Call them in for a relaxed interview, setting aside plenty of time to talk without any interruptions. Make it clear from the start that you're concerned and you want to help; you're not calling them in so you can read them the riot act.

Be straight with them. Tell them that they are one of your top performers and recently their work hasn't been up to its usual high standard. You're concerned and that's why you want to talk to them about it. The odds are that they will be relieved you've broached the subject. The likely reasons for going off form are:

- they are suffering from work-related stress (see page 54).
- they are going through a personal crisis (see page 60).

Follow the guidelines for whichever of these situations applies, and you should be well on your way to getting the problem sorted out.

A team member's absenteeism is getting worse

The important question here is whether the absenteeism is genuine. If it's getting worse, and without obvious reason, the concern is that the team member is swinging the lead. You need to ask yourself why anyone would do this. There is almost certainly some kind of problem at work – whether it's lack of motivation, boredom or some specific worry. Maybe they find the work too stressful, or perhaps they have a colleague who makes their working life unpleasant.

Talk to the person – in a relaxed, unhurried and private environment – and tell them you are concerned that they are increasingly absent. Ask them if there is a problem at work, and let them know you want to help. If they open up about such a problem, give them all the support you can while making it clear that taking time off is not the answer, and in future you expect them to come to you with problems rather than being absent from work.

In spite of your best efforts, some people simply won't give a good reason for taking time off. If you suspect they are malingering, there are things you can do:

- Call them at home to ask how they're feeling, and whether they expect to be at work the following day. Offer a visit from the company doctor if there is one. If they are frequently absent, call them at different times so they don't know when to expect the call. You could even call in the evening.

- If you catch someone malingering – down at the pub when they're supposed to be ill, for example – you have grounds for disciplining them. You may even be entitled to dismiss them.

- If you can't prove that they aren't really ill, make sure they give you a doctor's note. Ask them to see a doctor approved by the company (you can't force them to do this).

- If they refuse to give you a good reason, let them know that you will have to make a decision on how to proceed on the basis of the available facts. Warn them that you may decide to dismiss them (check your company's legal position before you go ahead with this).

- See also: 'One of your team is suffering from work-related stress', page 54, 'One of your team is going through a personal crisis', page 60, 'A top performer suddenly goes off form', page 69 and 'A member of staff seems impossible to motivate', page 80.

One of your team members is underperforming mildly

You don't want to discipline them, but you need them to improve – the key to this particular problem is to move fast. As soon as you think there might be a problem, tackle it straight away. Don't wait until you're certain there's a disciplinary matter to deal with. There are several good reasons for this:

- It's far easier to tackle someone over a small, minor problem than over a persistent, major one. If they are trying to get away with something they shouldn't, an early and relatively low-key warning could be all it takes to make them see that it's not worth pursuing because they *won't* get away with it. A quiet conversation to let them know you've noticed and you're concerned is probably all you need to get them back on track. If you leave it until later on, you'll have a much tougher interview to face.

- Some disruptive behaviour is habit forming. Take the example of letting deadlines slip. Someone may start by finding that you never seem to notice when they deliver work a day or two late. After a while they stop feeling guilty about it and stop trying so hard to be on time. Still you give no comment. By now they're in the habit of delivering work late routinely, and when you finally broach the subject with them they find it quite difficult to pull back on their deadlines. It's not really fair on the person if you don't deal with the problem straight away. If you've let them get away with missing their targets for three months they can quite reasonably have concluded that it was OK to do so. Suddenly your trying to tell them it's not.

- If someone is underperforming it's likely to affect the rest of the team. They will be frustrated that one person is getting away with something they shouldn't, or they'll be annoyed that they are carrying, or covering up for, one of the team. You need to deal with the problem quickly before these resentments have time to build up.

> "If someone is underperforming it's likely to affect the rest of the team".

One of your team resigns impulsively

To explain this problem I've used a specific example. Imagine one of your quality inspectors overlooks a batch of goods. After despatch, it turns out that they were faulty and have to be recalled and replaced. When this becomes clear, your quality inspector hands in their notice saying they feel they ought to resign. What should you do? Arrange to see them and:

- start by asking them to sit down. This makes it harder for them to walk out in the middle of the discussion.

- don't go over the whole episode again, or get upset or angry.

- discuss the resignation and not the original issue. Let them know that you feel it's unnecessary by saying something like, 'You made a mistake, but that's how we all learn. I don't expect it to happen again. You've been happy in the job until now, and I've been very satisfied with your performance.'

- offer to help, for example by training all the quality inspectors in company inspection systems.

- don't allow the resignation to push you into withdrawing any warnings, or to suggest they've done nothing wrong when you both know they have. If they are trying to use the resignation as leverage for this purpose, you may in the end have to call their bluff. Don't make concessions, but tell them you'll give them a week to retract their resignation if they'd like to before you start advertising for someone to replace them.

A weak member of the team thinks they are really good at the job

It doesn't so much matter what this person thinks – it's the poor performance you have to tackle. The aim is not to make them see that they are a weak performer, but to get them to be as effective as they think they are. So you deal with them pretty much as you would any other weak member of the team.

Don't label them as a strong or weak performer – you'll just get into an unhelpful debate with them and either lose or demoralize them completely. Simply focus on their performance. Make sure you set extremely clear targets

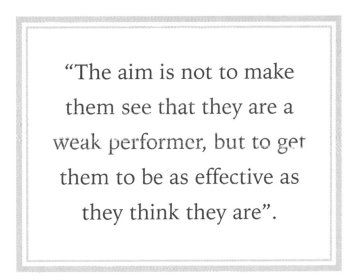

"The aim is not to make them see that they are a weak performer, but to get them to be as effective as they think they are".

and standards, which they agree to. Get these in writing if necessary. Make sure that these targets include failure standards, either implicitly or explicitly. That way, the team member can't miss targets or fall below standard without acknowledging that their performance wasn't up to scratch. This particularly applies if you have one of those people who are good in many ways but poor in one or two critical respects. You need to make them see that their performance is not up to scratch, however good the work if, for example, it is always delivered late, or is regularly peppered with minor errors. Be clear from the start that the target will not be met unless the work is on time, or unless it is error-free.

Now you have the tools to deal with poor performance without the team member being able to wriggle out of it and claim they've met their targets when they haven't. Once these failings in performances have been eliminated, they should be as good at the job as they believe they are.

A team member doesn't get on with the rest of the department

In a sense, your team member isn't doing the job properly if they can't get on with other people. They don't have to be particularly popular, but if they are so difficult or unpleasant that it causes a problem for the rest of the team, it's getting in the way of them doing the job effectively. It is everyone's job to contribute to a reasonable working relationship with their colleagues.

- Identify what it is precisely about this person that makes them hard to get on with. Concentrate on their behaviour and not their personality. Are their comments rude or overcritical, do they sulk if they don't get their own way or do they refuse to help their colleagues out?

- Call the person in for a private meeting. Don't discipline them formally, but make it clear that this is a work issue that needs to be sorted out because it's affecting the performance of the department.

- Let them know what the problem is. Don't label the person by saying 'You're a whinger' – simply discuss their behaviour: 'When you complain excessively it demoralizes people around you'. Have examples of this ready in case they challenge you. Use the principles of feedback (page 146).

- Don't give the person a persecution complex. There's no need to say, 'Everyone in the department has complained about you.' It's enough to be clear that *you* consider it a problem.

- Be aware that many people have been the same way for so many years that they may be completely unaware of how others perceive them. It may never have occurred to them that they overcriticize or are rude, and this may be a revelation to them. So be kind but firm. Don't shatter their self-confidence, but let them know that their behaviour must change.

One of your team is good but in the wrong job

This can happen surprisingly often. You really want the person on your team as they're a good, hard worker with lots of talent. The trouble is, their best talents don't coincide with the talents required for the job they are in.

- If your instinct tells you that you don't want to lose this person, then don't.

- Talk to the person concerned and explain that you don't feel they're suited to the job, but you believe in them and their abilities and you'd like them to stay with the organization. The chances are they'll be relieved to hear this – people know when they're in the wrong job, and they don't enjoy the feeling that they're not doing as well as they should.

- Ask the person if they have any ideas as to how they could contribute better to the organization. They may well have thought about this and may come up with interesting ideas. For example, they may say, 'What I really feel happy with is dealing with people. And I often think it would be useful if we had an internal liaison officer. I'd love to do that job.'

- Remember that the ideal job for this person may be in a different department to your own.

- Between you, find another job that suits the person better. It may mean them staying where they are for a few months until the budget is available for a new post, or someone vacates another post.

- Just occasionally, particularly in a small company, it can be impossible to find another post for someone. In that case, you (and they) have to decide whether it's better for them to stay in the wrong job, or to leave.

- If they choose to leave, or if you have to ask them to look for another job, be very supportive. Make it clear that you think they are talented, and it was a mistake appointing them to that post. Give them any time off they need for interviews, promise them glowing references and let them know that if any suitable post comes up in the future you'll contact them and see if they are interested. Treat them as well as you can to make sure they leave with positive feelings about the organization.

> "If your instinct tells you that you don't want to lose this person, then don't".

A member of staff seems impossible to motivate

Everyone can be motivated by something. The biggest mistake many managers make is to assume that everyone is motivated by the same things. Money and status are generally recognized as being key motivators, but they don't do it for everyone. You may have someone on your team who is looking for a different kind of incentive. All of the following are common motivators, and not everyone responds to all of them:

- money
- security
- status
- responsibility
- challenge.

On top of these, you can improve just about anyone's motivation if you give them:

- recognition – plenty of appreciation, thanks and praise when they perform well

- job satisfaction – they need to feel they can do the job well (you may need to train them), and to understand how their work fits into the scheme of things. Make sure they understand why their part of the process is essential to the organization as a whole

- involvement – tell them what's going on in the organization. Ask for their ideas, help or suggestions. And let them see that you are listening to them.

Just occasionally you may find you have someone on your team who doesn't respond to any kind of motivation you are in a position to provide. If this is the case you will have to talk to them about their poor performance, and ask them what would make them feel more enthusiastic about work. Ultimately, you may need to warn them that there is no place on your team for someone who doesn't want to be there.

Someone on the team has a persistently negative attitude

When someone says, 'It'll never work' it's extremely frustrating as well as being unconstructive. On the other hand, the pessimists are often the ones who stop the team from making mistakes. But they need careful handling if you are to exploit their ability to spot flaws, and stop them dragging the team down.

- When they express a negative view, ask them to make it specific: why won't it work? Are they guessing or are they basing their assessment on the facts? Is it just a hunch or do they have previous experience of this sort of thing? Be firm about getting them to be precise about which part of the project will create difficulties and why.

- Ask them how they think the problem can be resolved. Again, get them to be specific; don't settle for 'I don't know – the whole thing looks like a waste of time to me'.

- Pessimists are often afraid of failure, and therefore avoid taking risks. They try to stop the whole team taking risks as well by adopting such a negative viewpoint. Try asking them to tell you what they think the worst possible scenario could be as a result of following the course of action under discussion. This process often helps them to get their feelings in perspective.

- Remove their fear of failure by relieving them of as much responsibility as possible. Then, even if the project does fail, it won't be *their* failure. Either tell them you will take responsibility for the decision, or make it clear that

> "Pessimists are often afraid of failure, and therefore avoid taking risks".

the team as a whole is responsible (which dilutes their personal ownership of the project). Often, with this burden lifted, pessimists can become helpful contributors – although you have to realize they will never become optimists.

You decide you really don't like one of your team

Oh dear. You don't expect everyone on your team to be your best mate, but you do hope that you'd basically like them. You can't get rid of someone just because you don't like them, but working with them is no fun. If they're unpopular generally, they'll probably leave sooner or later – they'll sense they're not liked and they won't want to stay. But what if it's not everyone who dislikes them? What if it's just you?

If the problem is performance-related, you can do something about it. Maybe you dislike their negativity. You'll never turn such a person into an unbounded optimist, but you can reduce the impact of their negative attitude. Use feedback (see page 146) to resolve this kind of problem.

When your dislike stems purely from personality differences, and can't be blamed on their performance, your best bet is to minimize contact with them:

- give them projects where they can be fairly autonomous
- allocate them an office or desk well away from yours
- send them on frequent business trips
- allow them to work from home some of the time.

These kinds of measures will help a great deal. However, don't make it obvious why you're using them. The last thing you want is to make this person feel victimized, or to be guilty of letting the team see that you don't like them. It's not their fault, after all. Even if it galls, offer such things as business trips or working from home as positive perks or rewards. And, if you move their office away from yours, either have a damn good reason ('It's a bigger, smarter office for you to entertain clients in'), or have a team office or desk reshuffle so that no one realizes what you're up to.

In the end, although these measures will help, you're going to have to learn to live with the person. Many people find the best technique in this situation is to find at least something about the person that they like. If you can do that, things will be a lot easier for you.

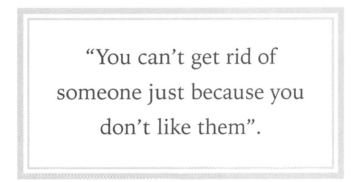

"You can't get rid of someone just because you don't like them".

You realize you've hired a complete nutter

Uh-oh! They looked great at the interview – bright and keen. Now you realize that was all neurotic energy. Maybe they get hysterical really easily. Or perhaps they're convinced you're always talking about them behind their back. There comes a point where wacky behaviour becomes seriously loopy. What can you do when you have a fruitcake on the team?

Are you alone?

To begin with, you need to assess whether this person really is a nutter, or whether you're the only one that thinks they are. You can have a quiet word with your own close colleagues, but don't ask *their* colleagues directly. If it gets back to them they really will have cause to feel paranoid. You'll soon know if your team think one of their colleagues is just too off the wall.

If it is only you who thinks they're a nutter – maybe everyone else just thinks they're slightly odd – I'm afraid you're going to have to learn to live with it, and learn a useful lesson about improving your recruitment skills. However, you can use feedback (see page 146) to deal with any specific problems. You might also find it helpful to look at 'You decide you really don't like one of your team', page 84.

Controlling the lunatic tendency

If it seems that many or even most people agree that this person's behaviour needs dealing with, you can take action.

- If you think this person has a genuine mental health problem, call them in for a private chat. Let them know that you feel they're not happy and might benefit from talking to someone. Offer them workplace counselling if it's available, or offer to support them if they want to find outside help. You could, for example, give them time off.

- If they just have a bizarre personality, you won't help by telling them so. There's nothing they can do. However, you can identify which part of their behaviour is causing problems and deal with that. Maybe they are demanding too much of your time, or perhaps they are over-emotional. You can use feedback (page 146) to tackle and alleviate this kind of problem.

- If you really want to get shot of your resident nutter, there's a good chance they're not really enjoying working for you. If you feel this is the case, talk to them and suggest that they don't seem happy. Tell them you feel you may have made a mistake employing them as the company culture doesn't seem to suit them. Suggest that if they would like to find another job you would understand entirely and will support them as much as you can.

You are asked to give a reference for a complete nutter

If the nutter is leaving you because you suggested they might be happier elsewhere, it really doesn't seem right to scupper their chances of finding another job by telling any prospective employer that the person they want to employ is a loony. At the same time, you don't really want to land the prospective employer in the same position as you.

The only fair course is to steer a middle line. Don't comment on their personality but focus purely on their performance. Be minimal – just stick to punctuality and attendance if you can – and don't make any negative comments. If the employer calls you for a telephone reference and pressures you to say more, you can say that the company culture didn't seem to suit them. Leave it at that.

One of your team is in disgrace

This is unlikely to happen in a well motivated and successful team, but occasionally one of your team members may be disciplined for drunkenness, pilfering or some other offence that the rest of the team knows about. Or they may have been responsible for a serious and negligent mistake that has damaged the team.

- Deal with the situation in the appropriate way, by disciplining the team member or giving them a warning.

- Then treat them exactly as normal and let it be seen by the rest of the team that you consider that the matter has been dealt with and that things are back to normal.

Someone on your team is having an affair

One of your team is having a fling with one of the directors of the company or two married team members are having an affair. What do you do about it?

The good news is that 95 per cent of the time you do absolutely nothing. It's none of your business. It only becomes your business if it interferes with the team and its work. In this instance it's a simple matter of taking the person – or people – on one side and letting them know that you're not happy about the effect this is having on the team. If two team members are involved talk to them separately, not together, since each one is independently contributing to the problem. They might also feel inhibited and unable to talk freely in front of each other.

Behave as though the affairs weren't happening, in terms of how you treat the people concerned. If the rest of the team think that one of their colleagues suddenly has more clout with you just because they have a special relationship with a member of senior management, you will lose the loyalty of the rest of your team. Let everyone see that it makes no difference and there shouldn't be a problem.

If they split up

The other occasional, and certainly uncomfortable, situation you may encounter is when two of your team have a relationship with each other and then split up acrimoniously. Worse still, the rest of the team may even take sides. Again, talk to the two people separately and let them know that they are damaging the team and that they must resolve things at least while they are at work. Tell them you hold them at least partly responsible if other members of the team take sides. Then speak to the other members of the team one at a time, briefly. Say to them, 'It's none of our business what is going on privately between Robin and Kim, but I am making it clear to everyone on the team, including them, that it mustn't get in the way of work. If you have an opinion on the subject, I'd like you to forget about it during working hours. I understand that this may not always seem easy, but it's important for the good of the team.'

If the atmosphere is still strained after this, try to keep the two of them physically apart for a while by sending them off on business trips, rerostering or whatever. They'll probably be grateful. The problem should subside fairly quickly – if they really find it impossible to work together in the long term one of them will probably leave or ask for a transfer anyway.

You've sacked someone and you have to tell the rest of the team

As a manager you should have been trained in dismissal procedures. But what about breaking the news to everyone else? As soon as the person you've dismissed has gone, call the team together.

- Don't give them any confidential information about their ex-colleague's misbehaviour but tell them that you regret that it had to happen and there was nothing personal in your decision. Explain that you dismissed the person because their presence in the team was preventing the whole team from achieving its full potential – they were probably all well aware of this and will understand. If it's appropriate point out that the person was not a failure in themselves, they were merely unsuitable for the team.

- Let them know that you are confident that you were acting in the best interests of the team as a whole, and you are sure that they will now be even more successful. You feel that all the remaining members are valuable to the team and each has an important contribution to make.

One of your team has cost the company millions

They didn't read the small print, they agreed to too much or they said the wrong thing. Whatever the nature of the mistake, it's going to cost a fortune. The first thing to do, before you deal with the person concerned, is to see if you can find any way to undo the damage. Can you talk to the customer or supplier concerned, explain the problem and salvage anything? Maybe you can appeal to their better nature, if they have one.

Whether or not you can rescue the situation, you'll have to deal with the team member concerned. The critical thing here is to focus on the mistake and not on its consequences when it comes to dishing out punishment. If the mistake was seemingly minor and understandable, or perhaps the person who made it couldn't have known the consequences, then discipline them for a minor offence. It's just unfortunate that it turned out to be a costly mistake.

If, however, the mistake really should have been avoided, and the person concerned had the experience to know that, you'll need to be tougher in your response. For example, you should always read the small print in a contract, but when millions of pounds are involved, it's more important than ever. If your team member didn't bother to check the contract thoroughly, that's a serious and avoidable error.

If this kind of mistake is typical for this person – maybe you've had to discipline them for sloppy work before – this catastrophic error may be the final straw that leads you to sack them for poor performance.

Someone on your team repeatedly bends the rules

Most people who bend the rules do it to get results. Maybe they allow their staff to disregard health and safety guidelines in the interests of speed. Or perhaps they give suppliers more time in exchange for better discounts, thereby cutting restocking times dangerously fine.

The first thing to do is to consider open mindedly whether the rules really make sense. If a lot of people tend to bend them, it could be a sign that the rules are at fault. Even if they seem necessary – perhaps safety is at issue – is there another solution? Would different safety equipment give the same protection without taking so long to put in place? Assuming the rules are needed, you'll need to talk to the rule bender privately.

- Explain why the rules are necessary. Tell them that regardless of whether they agree with you, they must adhere to the rules or you will have to report them or give them a warning. Stand up to them. Don't accept the argument that bending the rules brings in better results.

> "Stand up to them. Don't accept the argument that bending the rules brings in better results".

- If you can, get their colleagues to help. Don't mention names, but bring up the subject at a team meeting. If you can get the rule bender's peers to agree that it's not worth compromising health and safety, for example, that may carry more weight than your own view.

- If you have several rule benders on your team, give them separate tasks to do. That way, you can split them up and work on them individually.

You have to discipline a team member who is also a friend

Begin the interview with some kind of businesslike gesture to signal that this is a formal meeting. You might close the door and ask them to sit down, for example.

- You can start by saying, 'I'm sure you realize that just because we're friends, I still have to treat you exactly as I do the rest of the team. I'm sure you wouldn't want me to do anything else.'

- Then carry on with the interview just as you would with anyone else, without reference to the friendship. If they refer to it, or speak to you with too much familiarity, stop them firmly with a remark such as, 'Let's keep this formal'.

If your team member can't or won't ignore the friendship during the interview, let them know you'll have to bring in a third party to sit in. If you have to do this, invite them to choose who it should be. If they won't, bring in one of their managers (either junior or senior to yourself) or someone from personnel. You can't just invite a colleague to sit in on their discipline interview without their permission – it must be someone who is entitled to be involved.

Someone on your team is drinking heavily

When someone is persistently drunk at work, you can generally dismiss them once you have been through the usual warnings and procedures without any effect. You can sometimes dismiss for a single incidence of drunkenness if:

- safety was endangered

- company property was endangered

- their behaviour while drunk was serious

. . . although you should always check your legal position.

It is more of a problem, however, when you don't want to sack them but just want them to stop drinking. Maybe they're otherwise an excellent performer. Perhaps they've only started drinking since the start of a personal problem that you're sympathetic to. What can you do?

The sooner you tackle this, the better. The longer they go on drinking at lunchtime (or whenever), the harder it will be for them to give it up. So deal with it as soon as you can see that it's more than a one-off.

- Call the person in for a private talk. Be blunt, but not aggressive. You can say something like, 'We need to talk about your drinking at lunchtime. How many drinks do you usually have during lunch?'

- Explain why their drinking is a problem: 'You're responsible for safety,' or 'Your team is losing respect for you,' or 'Your performance has deteriorated recently' or 'You may be over the limit when you drive your company car'.

- Remind them of the company rules about drunkenness at work, and tell them they will be the subject of disciplinary proceedings if the drinking doesn't stop.

- Let them know that, while you will take a firm line on drinking at work, you will support them if they need help giving up their lunchtime drinking. Maybe you could let them skip lunch and go home an hour early instead so they get no chance to drink. Or perhaps you could offer to have sandwiches brought in, or help to set the trend for team lunches at a local café instead of down the pub.

One of your team loses their driving licence, which they need to do the job

The first thing to do is to consider whether they can get the job done in any other way:

- Can they deal with customers and other contacts by phone?

- Could they travel by train, bus, cab or plane instead?

- Could they cut down travel, and have a driver when they do need to travel by car?

If it's really impossible for them to carry out the job without driving you will need to consider what to do next.

- You may be able to find them another position in the company.

- You should be able to dismiss them if the contract states that being able to drive is a condition of the job.

- If it's not their fault they lost their licence – perhaps they've been diagnosed with a medical condition – it would be advisable to take legal advice before sacking them. It would, in any case, reflect badly on the organization (and quite rightly) if you dismissed someone under such circumstances unless all other options had been exhausted.

- If they lost their licence through drink driving it would normally be advisable to sack them if driving is an essential part of their job.

It appears someone on your team has been stealing

This is a problem when you don't know who the guilty party is. Theft is a matter for the police; it's not your job to find the culprit although, clearly it *is* your job to do anything you can to help the police find them. The problems in the team arise when there is a suspicion that it is an inside job – one of your team may be the thief.

- You must carry on as normal. Pass on to the police, in confidence, any information you feel may be useful, and leave it at that. Keep your eyes open, but don't go rummaging in people's desks when they're not there or manically checking up on their petty cash records. They'll realize instantly what you're doing.

> "If your team members think for a moment that you don't trust them, it will do virtually irreparable damage to your relationship with them".

- If your team members think for a moment that you don't trust them, it will do virtually irreparable damage to your relationship with them. Then, when the culprit is caught, all the innocent members of your team (which may well be every one of them) will have to work with you knowing that you considered them all capable of theft. If you only suspect one or two of them, who turn out not to be guilty, your relationship with them will be even worse.

- Set your team an example. Until proven otherwise, your attitude must be 'None of my team would do this. We'll be vigilant but since none of us is guilty we shan't allow it to get in the way of our work.'

You find one of your team is on the fiddle

If a member of your team is pilfering, or worse, from the organization, this should be grounds for dismissal. However, in minor cases of pilfering you should take legal advice since there are times – especially in isolated incidents where there are mitigating circumstances – when you may not have a legitimate excuse to dismiss.

If you want to dismiss the person concerned, make sure you can prove that they are fiddling the organization. You don't want to find yourself at an industrial tribunal explaining that no one actually saw them do it but you reckon it's bound to have been them.

This kind of behaviour is sometimes a problem if you don't want to dismiss, and are unsure how to handle the person concerned. Suppose a very strong and able member of the team turns out occasionally to be using petrol paid for by the company for home use. Or maybe they are keeping their young child supplied with paper for drawing on from your stationery cupboard. You don't have to dismiss if you don't want to, but you need to discipline the person concerned and almost certainly give them a formal warning. Here are a few more points to consider:

- Make sure you are scrupulously fair. If you let someone off with a written warning, you could be in trouble if you later sack someone else for the same offence.

- Be aware of the signals you are sending out to everyone else. If you don't take the offence very seriously you are, in effect, telling everyone else that it's not a big deal if they steal from the organization.

- When someone fiddles the company they are guilty of a breach of good faith – which is a requirement of employees. Think carefully about whether you believe that this person is likely to breach your trust in some way again. If you feel they are a high risk, it might be wiser to dismiss them.

You discover one of your team members has a dodgy police record

Convictions are either spent or unspent. After a certain number of years (which varies according to the offence) a conviction is deemed to be spent. This means that it does not have to be declared and you have no right to ask about it. So if you do discover it by some chance, there's nothing you can – or should need to – do about it.

The real question is: what should you do if you discover one of your team has unspent convictions they didn't tell you about?

- Consider whether the conviction impinges on their suitability for the job in any way. The obvious example here is someone with a conviction for child abuse working with children. But there are plenty of others: a dangerous driving conviction, for example, would be relevant for someone who spends a lot of time on the road.

- Failure to tell you about an unspent conviction that is relevant in this way can constitute a breach of trust and may therefore be grounds for dismissal (but always take legal advice if you're thinking of dismissing someone for not telling you about unspent convictions).

- If the conviction was not relevant to this job, you don't necessarily have grounds to dismiss. But would you want to anyway? You'll need to talk to the person about the fact that they lied to you, but the conviction itself isn't necessarily the issue.

- Call the person in and follow your normal disciplinary procedure. Let them know you're very concerned that they lied or misled you during the selection process. Ask them to tell you why they lied, and to reassure you if they can that they haven't lied to you at any other time.

Bear in mind that all the above only applies if you asked them at selection – either on paper or in person – whether they had any unspent convictions. If you never asked, you have only yourself to blame if you find out later that they had a conviction you wish you'd known about. They can quite legitimately argue, 'You never asked'.

> "If you never asked, you have only yourself to blame if you find out later that they had a conviction you wish you'd known about".

One of your team gave false qualifications or references when they got the job

...and you've only just found out. Normally this is grounds for dismissal, as long as your offer of employment was subject to satisfactory references and qualifications. However, you don't have to dismiss if you don't want to.

- If the person is performing well in the job, you may be quite happy to continue employing them.

- Take into account, however, whether you feel your trust in them is detrimentally affected.

- It would be wise to discipline them at least, to make clear the seriousness of the offence. Even if it hasn't mattered in the long run, they still lied to you. And ask them to tell you if they have misinformed you about anything else – this is their chance to come clean.

> "If the person is performing well in the job, you may be quite happy to continue employing them".

Although this generally constitutes grounds for dismissal, it's always advisable to check your legal position. The person may have been with the company for a long time, the qualification they lied about hasn't been necessary to the job or they've performed satisfactorily – these points may well lead an industrial tribunal to question whether there is a need to dismiss the person.

CHAPTER 2

YOUR MANAGERS

You think your boss is rubbish

Bosses who are downright incompetent can make your life immensely difficult, especially when it reflects on you. The whole department may perform poorly as a result and you (and your team mates) miss out on bonuses, promotions and successes. The challenge is to make sure that others realize that you don't deserve to be tarred with the same brush as your boss.

- Get as much of your own contribution to the organization down in writing as you can. Instead of taking ideas to the boss verbally, write them down as proposals. These may only be a page long, but they're there in black and white. Now make sure they get seen outside the department. Copy them to anyone you can justify copying them to. You can tell your boss, 'I've copied this to despatch because I thought their input would be useful in helping us to schedule,' or 'I thought Mike could use this idea in his department, too, so I've emailed him a copy of my proposal'.

- Now do the same with any warnings you have to make. If you are concerned that a project is going off course, email your boss or send them a memo outlining your concerns and your recommendations for remedying the problem. Again, copy them wherever you can. Even if you can't, at least keep your own copies. Then when things go wrong, it will be clear it wasn't your fault. In fact, if the boss had listened to you, they wouldn't have gone wrong. And suppose the boss *does* take your advice? Better still – you have a success on your hands, and the paperwork shows it was all thanks to your intervention.

- Finally, get your achievements down in black and white, and circulated as widely as possible. You don't have to send round a memo saying, 'Aren't I brilliant? Look what I did!' You could email your boss with essential details of a big new contract you've just landed and copy it to other

> ## "Get as much of your own contribution to the organization down in writing as you can".

relevant departments. Just make sure it's clear that you were the one who landed the deal, came up with the idea or put in the hard work.

If your boss is incompetent, your aim should be to get promoted out of the department as soon as possible – or promoted into your boss's job. However, you don't want to make your boss feel threatened, or you will make a bad situation worse. So don't start trying to steal their job. It's only a matter of time before they move (or get moved) without your help, especially once you've made sure everyone knows that it's not you (and your colleagues) who is incompetent.

You don't like your boss

Mmm. The answer here, I'm afraid, is to put up or shut up. Many people leave jobs because they really aren't happy working for a boss they can't get on with. Most of them never regret it, either. It may be the boss's working style or it may be a matter of personalities. Either way, if you're unhappy, you need to think hard about what the point is of staying in the job. Unless one of you looks likely to get promoted or transferred soon, or your boss is already looking for another job, leaving is frequently the best option.

If it's not that bad, or you really don't want to leave, then you'll have to learn to live with the situation. Don't keep bitching about your boss behind their back – eventually they will find out and things will become more unpleasant than they were before. Your best bet is to:

- minimize contact with your boss – ask to work from home part time or do more business travelling, for example
- learn to like at least something about them – many people manage to do this very successfully and find their working lives become easier for it

If you decide to live with the problem for now, you can always change your mind later if it becomes intolerable.

The boss is picking on you personally

Maybe your boss is a great boss to most of the team, but not for you. Being singled out and picked on is deeply distressing; arguably worse than receiving the same treatment from a boss who dishes it out to everybody.

The first step is to talk to your colleagues if you can. See if they are aware of your problem, and enlist their support if you can. If they back you up when the boss is picking on you, it will make it obvious that they can see what the boss is up to – which may act as a deterrent.

The first step is to talk to your boss. Be assertive and non-confrontational and try to find out why they're picking on you. Don't put it in these terms; instead tell them you get the feeling that they are displeased with something you're doing, or failing to do. Ask them what you can do to resolve things. If there's a specific cause, the boss will probably tell you in response to this and you can take steps to change things. If the cause is more to do with personalities, or maybe jealousy on your boss's part, you won't get a clear response. But highlighting the problem may well persuade them to lay off you.

Your boss is prejudiced against you

When people judge you wrongly for something you have no control over, it is extremely frustrating. When it's your boss, it can also damage your career. Whether they are sexist, racist, ageist or classist – or anything else – you need to tackle the problem.

Meeting with your boss for a calm discussion of the problem can be very helpful, forcing your boss to acknowledge that your performance is not affected by your age, gender, race or any other similar factor. But alongside this, there are some other steps you can take to help your case.

- Don't get involved in an argument with your boss about their prejudice. Decline to discuss whether women are better than men, whether experience or youth is better, and so on. You will only reinforce their prejudice. You're not going to change your mind after such a debate, and it's no more likely that they will.

- Show by example. Volunteer for tasks that will prove your point, and behave in ways that will undermine their prejudice. For example, if your boss is a sexist woman who thinks all men are dunderheads, take on a task requiring delicate diplomacy when you get the chance, and let her see you can handle it. If you're a lot older than your boss, don't be a stick-in-the-mud – rather let them see that older people can be creative and open to new ideas. When you decide to ask for a meeting about the problem with your boss, you'll be armed with examples that contradict their prejudice.

- At the same time, don't inadvertently reinforce their views. If you're a woman with a sexist boss, don't ask him to change the light bulb for you.

> "Volunteer for tasks that will prove your point, and behave in ways that will undermine their prejudice".

It may not have anything to do with your ability to do the job, but it will convince him women are pathetic – even if you were only asking because he's six inches taller than you. You don't want to arm your boss with examples to use at the meeting. When you ask for examples of how your work is detrimentally affected by your being a woman/being over 50/being public school educated/being black/being gay or whatever your boss's prejudice is, you want them to be unable to cite any example.

Of course, you always have the option here of going to your boss's boss with a complaint (or even taking more extreme legal action if you believe you have a case). A meeting with the boss is always worth trying first, but if your boss is unresponsive is it worth going over their head? Only you can decide on the answer to this, but here are a few factors to take into account:

- Is your boss's boss likely to be sympathetic – or, if not, is there a personnel department that you could go to instead?

- How is your boss likely to respond? *Their* boss can't do anything useful without talking to them, so it's no good thinking they won't find out. Is it likely to pull them up short, or more likely to make them resentful towards you?

- Have you any firm evidence of their treating you in a prejudiced fashion? If not, you have relatively little chance of success unless you encounter someone sympathetic who knows your boss well enough to know you're being honest.

- Do you have colleagues who will vouch for the prejudiced treatment you say you've been receiving from your boss?

- How much do you want this job? I'm not suggesting you should say nothing, but the action you take may be affected by your answer to this question. If the job's become unbearable, you might as well take drastic action since you have nothing to lose. If the reaction makes things worse, you'll be happy to leave. But if you thoroughly enjoy the job, apart from your boss's attitude, you'll want to try more circumspect approaches first.

Your boss expects you to be a workaholic

When you have family commitments you simply can't keep working late. If your boss wants to work 18 hours a day it's really not your problem. But if you're expected to join in it can be a big problem. And the more of your colleagues that play ball, the more isolated you will feel if you complain.

If it's not too late already, don't start working long hours. It's a lot easier to say no in the first place than to get fed up after a few months and try cutting your workload down by several hours a week. There are some other steps to consider.

- Talk to your boss. If you can get the support of your team mates, this will be even more effective. But don't make it look like a mutiny; just a collective request for a rethink on the hours your department works. Explain that when you took this job on, you were led to believe the working hours were nine to five (or whatever they're supposed to be – check your contract to make sure of your facts). Don't come across as a jobsworth; you can say that you understand that it's not realistic to expect to leave work on the dot of five every day, but that working late seems to have become the norm and it's making you feel demoralized and demotivated. Point out that you have family commitments too.

- Don't allow your boss to intimidate you into working unreasonably long hours. You are not paid to work these hours, so you have the right to refuse. Your boss has to recognize that you work extra hours out of goodwill, and you can be assertive and explain that you are not happy giving the organization so many extra hours for nothing, and you intend to reduce the work you do outside office hours.

> ## "Don't allow your boss to intimidate you into working unreasonably long hours".

- If you want to tell your boss why working late or at weekends interferes with family commitments, it may help them realize that you're not being difficult for the sake of it – you really have a problem.

- The biggest problem for your boss, in practical terms, will be that if you reduce your hours you will necessarily reduce the amount of work you get through each week. So do whatever you can to help. Improve your time management skills, delegate what you can and find ways to streamline tasks. You might discuss this option with your boss, and let them know you're aiming to reduce your hours without your work suffering.

- You can often cut your hours without reference to the boss. If they notice you're now knocking off at six instead of eight each evening, and try to give you an extra few hours work a week to fill in the time, make it clear you've improved your effectiveness for your own benefit, not theirs.

- Expect it to take time to cut down your hours. Tell your boss, for example, that when your current project is completed at the end of next month, you intend to avoid working such long hours again. You're not trying to get out of your existing workload, you're just planning to reduce it by natural wastage. You may need to do this in several stages, depending on the options and how many hours you're trying to cut.

You'll need to recognize that your boss isn't likely to be happy with you working nine to five if no one else does. It might seem like plenty to you, but they'll see you as lazy. If you are otherwise happy with the job, and want to stay, find a reasonable compromise. Maybe you could work half an hour late each day, with the occasional late evening for a special reason. Be prepared, however, for your boss's constant pressure to increase this, and be ready to decline tasks that won't fit into the working hours you're happy with.

Your boss seems to think you're permanently on call

If your boss is inclined to call you up out of hours, or even on holiday, make it impossible for them:

- don't give them your number, or only give them your mobile number and turn it off whenever you can

- leave your answering machine on at home, or get someone else to answer calls. Make it clear you consider it an invasion of privacy being called out of hours

- tell them the place you're holidaying doesn't have a phone – or be straight and tell them it does but you're not giving them the number

- brief family and colleagues not to put the boss in touch with you.

Your boss is having a tough time and is taking it out on you

This is inexcusable, no matter what pressure your boss is under. What's more, if this isn't their usual behaviour, they probably know deep down that it's unacceptable. Any boss may have the odd bad day when they're a bit prickly or snappy, and you should be able to ignore it, but a sustained change in behaviour over a significant period of time needs remedying.

When your boss is giving you a hard time, respond coolly but assertively. Don't snap back or retaliate in kind, but make it clear that you're not prepared to be spoken to rudely or shouted at. The simplest way to do this is simply to say, 'Please don't shout at me'. A boss who is only treating you like this because they are under stress will most probably be shocked to realize how rude they are being, and will be pulled up short by such a response.

If the problem persists, talk to your boss in private. Let them know how you feel when they take their emotions out on you. Be reasonable and constructive – don't make accusations. Approach the issue from your own

"Sustained change in behaviour over a significant period of time needs remedying".

perspective, expressing the fact that you are upset and concerned by their behaviour. Once they realize how serious the problem is becoming, they should take action.

Your boss's personal stress – whether home- or work-related – is none of your business. They may not want to talk about it, and they may not want to admit that it is the cause of their changed behaviour. That would suggest that they can't cope with the stress (it may be true, but that's beside the point). So don't bring up the subject. After all, the cause of their behaviour isn't the issue – it's the behaviour itself you need to address – so it's not actually relevant.

Your boss is having a tough time and bursts into tears in front of you

Whether your boss has just been bawled out by the MD, or whether they are going through a particularly horrendous divorce, what do you do if they burst into tears in front of you? Here are a few guidelines:

- Drop the boss/subordinate relationship for the duration, and treat them as you would any fellow human being who is upset.

- If you think they might prefer you not to be there, ask them, 'Would you prefer me to leave?' If you don't get a direct answer, stay with them unless the signals to go are strong.

- Let them talk, and you do the listening.

- Don't give them any advice unless they specifically ask for it, and preferably not then either.

- Next time you see your boss you can ask, 'How are you feeling?' but don't make a big thing of it, or ask them repeatedly, unless they encourage it. They may well be embarrassed later, and be uncomfortable with any reference to it.

- No matter what they say or do, don't mention the incident to anyone else in or connected with the organization. Your boss will appreciate and respect your ability to maintain their confidence, and it will build their trust in you. Betraying their confidence will do serious damage to your relationship.

> "Treat them as you would any fellow human being who is upset".

- Unless your boss is also a close friend, don't mention the incident to them again unless they bring it up first. Most particularly, don't use it as any kind of emotional leverage, in other words don't remind them how sympathetic you were just as you're asking for a day off, or imply that they owe you a favour.

Your boss takes credit for your ideas

This is not only infuriating, it's also damaging to your career. If your good ideas aren't recognized as your own, how can you be rewarded for them? You need to take action to make sure you get the credit you deserve.

- Keep records of your ideas and suggestions, and notes of relevant meetings with your boss. Send them memos and emails in order to elicit a written response. For example, send them an email saying, 'As I promised during our meeting about my idea for developing a motorized pushchair, here are the figures . . .'. Any reply that doesn't argue with your mention of its being your idea clearly acknowledges the fact that it is.

- Get your ideas down as a formal proposal, with your name on the cover page and the date.

- Let other people know about your ideas, either verbally or by copying to them anything you can justify, including your proposal.

- As well as getting your ideas and successes down in writing yourself, try to elicit – an keep on file – any outside evidence to back you up. Testimonials from customers, emails from other managers offering thanks or praise, statistics showing how things have improved since you introduced your idea . . . all these go to show that the credit should be yours.

- After the idea has been proved a success, blow your own trumpet as much as you can. Let people know how pleased you are that your idea turned out to be a winner. While senior management may be the group you most want to notice you and recognize the idea as your own, it's worth telling anyone just to get your success widely circulated. So tell colleagues in other departments as well as your own, managers of other departments and so on.

- In order to avoid riling your boss, give them credit (even if you're not sure they really deserve it) for encouraging your idea. You may even feel you can send an email or memo to your boss's boss, saying how grateful you were for your boss's support for your idea.

> "If your good ideas aren't recognized as your own, how can you be rewarded for them?"

Your boss blames you for their mistake

None of us likes being blamed at the best of times, and being blamed for someone else's mistakes is particularly galling. But, more than that, it can be deeply damaging to your career.

- For a start, if your boss makes a habit of this, put your achievements down in writing, as you would for a boss who takes credit for your ideas (see page 125). That way you'll have the details when you need them – appraisals, promotion interviews and so on. If your boss tries to blame you in private, draw their attention to the relevant paperwork.

- Encourage your boss to put instructions to you in writing. If you encounter problems with this, simply email them saying, for example, 'Before I launch into this, can I clarify your instructions? You've asked me to . . .'. They need only send back an email saying, 'Yes' to have committed themselves on paper.

- Don't try to put the blame back on your boss, reasonable though it might seem. If you say, 'It wasn't my fault, it was yours, and I can prove it' you may make your point, but you'll do serious damage to your working relationship. Your boss probably knows perfectly well it was their fault – that's why they're so desperate to palm the blame off on to you. Instead, use the word 'we' a lot, as in 'We certainly didn't get the results we wanted . . .', or 'With hindsight, we'd have done better to set the schedule further in advance . . .' and then focus on solutions. Don't accept the blame, just aim to avoid pointing fingers at all and move on to the next stage.

- If your boss blames you for their mistakes in public, don't try to pass the blame back to them in front of everyone else. It may be fair, but it won't work. Most people won't be able to tell which of you is telling the truth, and the result will be that you'll look petty and your boss will be furious with you. Instead, take the blame, but do it collectively, using that word 'we' a lot: 'There's no denying we misjudged this one . . .'.

- Now focus on the solution, outlining how you think the problem can be solved, and what you can do to help. Drop the 'we' for this bit, and talk about yourself as 'I' when it comes to finding solutions and rescuing disasters.

You think your boss has made a major mistake

What you do here depends rather on the nature of the mistake. If drawing attention to the mistake won't help, there's no point in doing it. This would apply when it's too late to salvage it and, for example, if:

- your boss doesn't welcome constructive criticism

- you aren't implicated in the mistake

- no one is likely to notice anyway.

If it isn't too late to put the mistake right, however, you should try to – even if you don't think it will work. It's important to be seen to have realized the problem and tried to remedy it. So even if you are convinced your boss won't listen, tell them anyway. Do it in writing – email will do – so you have a permanent record.

If your boss really doesn't want to know, you may be able to develop some kind of contingency for when the mistake finally comes to light. Suppose your boss has switched to a new supplier who you think is very unreliable. You reckon that when the next rush order goes through they will let you down badly. You could at least get quotes and timescales from other suppliers so that when your boss's supplier admits they can't fulfil the order on time, you've got another supplier lined up.

If your boss is open enough to listen to you, tell them that you think they've made a mistake (only don't phrase it so bluntly) even if it's too late to salvage it. At least they will have time to prepare their response when the mistake is revealed, and they'll appreciate you giving them that time.

If your boss is likely to blame you when the mistake comes to light, see 'Your boss blames you for their mistake', on page 127.

You think your boss is about to make a major mistake

It's essential that you warn your boss if you think they're about to cock up big time. Even if you don't expect them to listen, at least you'll put yourself out of the firing line. Your primary aim is to prevent the mistake, but your fallback position should be to make sure that if it *does* happen, at least you won't get blamed.

Talk to your boss as diplomatically as you can. Don't say, 'I think you're making a big mistake,' say something like, 'I'm concerned about the Belton's order. Can I talk to you about it?' Then tell them what you fear will happen. Make sure that you don't have this conversation until you have an alternative course of action to recommend, even if the alternative is simply to do nothing at all. There's no point trying to persuade your boss to change course if every other option looks even worse.

Unless your boss instantly says, 'You're absolutely right! Thank goodness you saved me from a dreadful mistake,' you should also put your views in writing to them. You can email them saying, 'To recap what we discussed this morning . . .'. The point of this is to give you written evidence, should you need it, that you weren't part of the mistake. It's not to wave under the boss's nose in three months time chanting, 'Told you so! Told you so!' But if things get sticky, and especially if the boss tries to blame you, you may need it. (See also, 'Your boss blames you for their mistake', page 131.)

You've got two bosses who both expect you to work full time for them

The first step to handling multiple bosses is to get them talking to each other. Explain that you don't want to let either of them down, and that the best way to achieve this is for them to agree between them what your priorities should be. So if you know that one of them has a big project coming up, or another is going to be short staffed until they fill that vacancy, anticipate trouble and ask them to meet in advance to discuss how much of your time should be allocated to each of them. Ideally, arrange to be at the meeting yourself too if you can.

Anticipate trouble

The next stage is to anticipate shorter term trouble yourself. If one of your bosses gives you a time consuming task to do, ask them straight away to clear it with the other, or do so yourself. As soon as you can see your time is about to be filled without gaps for the next few days, make sure everyone is aware of the situation. That way, when you tell your second boss your schedule has just been filled they can say, for example, 'Ah. I'm going to need you to chase up those missing orders for me tomorrow morning. I'll talk to Janet now and see if she can spare you for half a day.'

This also has the advantage of keeping your bosses regularly reminded that they are not the only person you work for. Even on those occasions when they don't have a problem with your workload being filled by another boss, they'll still be reminded that they can't ever take your availability for granted.

Last minute hiccups

Keeping your bosses in touch with each other and anticipating trouble will make a big difference. But there will still be times when one of your bosses tries to insist that you carry out a task that you simply don't have time for. Suppose they demand that you chase up the missing orders today, but that would mean you wouldn't get your other boss's research done by the time you agreed. The answer here is to insist that they sort it out among themselves. Make sure that:

- they do not expect you to take responsibility for deciding whose work gets finished late

- they don't blame you for the situation they've got themselves into

- they don't use you as a go-between.

As a default setting, explain that you have to operate on a 'first come, first served' basis. The work you've already agreed to takes priority. You're happy to change this if everyone agrees to the change, but you need this boss to go away, clear any changes to your priorities with your other boss and then let you know. Until you're told that *they* have collectively agreed a change, you'll carry on as planned.

Unless you trust your bosses absolutely, make sure that the other boss really has agreed to change your priorities. The last thing you want is Janet saying, 'I've spoken to Paul, and he says he can wait until Thursday for you to chase the orders' only to have Paul demand to know why it hasn't been done on Wednesday. When you tell him what Janet said he insists he said no such thing, and blames you for changing your priorities without consulting him. So unless you trust her absolutely, tell Janet to get Paul to let you know – phone or email you if he's out of the office – that it's OK to give priority to her work.

As with the boss who tries to give you too much work, you have to be firm here. It is not your responsibility to make their decisions for them about priorities. So if they tell you that their work is desperately urgent and they can't get hold of your other boss, that's their problem. Be polite but firm: 'I'm sorry, but I can't let Paul down. If you can't contact him then I'm afraid I'll have to do his work first as I agreed with him.' Keep repeating it until they get the message. And you can point out that you'd do the same for them if the situation were reversed. Make sure that you would, too – don't ever show favouritism in your professional relationships with your bosses.

You may be wondering – and you will be if this applies to you – what happens when one of your bosses is senior enough to overrule the other. When Janet says, 'I don't care what Paul says; I'm overruling him. Get this urgent research done first and then chase his orders when you've finished this,' what do you do?

The answer is still the same: it's not your responsibility to sort out *their* problems. If Janet is authorized to overrule Paul, you'd better do as she tells you. Then get in touch with Paul and tell him the situation. Be firm if necessary and make it clear that if he's not happy you may sympathize but there's nothing you can do. If he wants to sort it out, he'll have to talk to Janet. If he asks you to talk to her, refuse politely: 'No, the only way to sort it out is for you to talk to her directly. I'll just end up as a go-between and nothing will get resolved. If you want her to change her mind, you'll have to talk to her.'

If you are consistently assertive with your bosses when problems crop up, and you refuse to get drawn into making decisions for them or acting as go-between, they'll soon learn to stop asking you to take on responsibility for prioritizing between them. They will have to be united in the instructions, and the changes, that they give you. And your stress levels will drop wonderfully – and deservedly – as a result.

You are given targets you know are unrealistic

This is immensely demoralizing, quite apart from the fact that you risk looking like a failure when you inevitably fail to meet your targets. You have to tackle this with your boss.

- Targets should always be agreed between you and your boss, not imposed from above. Your boss clearly doesn't realize this. So you'll need to educate them.

- Point out to your boss when they set you a task that they are asking for the impossible. Tell them, 'I can do that to the standard you want, but not by the end of May. If you want it completed then, I'll have to compromise elsewhere.'

- Get them to recognize the problem in advance and help find a workable solution, rather than waiting until afterwards to complain that the brief was impossible. To do this, you will need to come up with very clear justifications for your argument that the target is unrealistic. Collect together all the data, schedules and advice you need to demonstrate to your boss why you can't meet it.

- If your boss tries to insist that you do it (which will be very rare if you've put together a good case for adjusting the target), put in writing why you feel the target is unfeasible. As time progresses, give them regular written updates warning them that you are behind schedule, and reiterating why this has happened.

- Throughout the process, do your genuine best to meet the target. The aim is not to prove the boss wrong, but merely to cover your back if their demands are unreasonable. Sometimes they may be realistic with the targets they impose, and you should be able to recognize when this is the case.

Your boss expects you to do something illegal

Only you can decide what you are or aren't prepared to do for your boss. But breaking the law is extremely inadvisable, quite apart from the ethical issues involved. If you get caught it will be no defence that your boss told you to do it. Your career could be jeopardized if you go ahead.

- Once you decide you're not prepared to break the law, go to your boss. Don't moralize or lecture them; simply tell them you are uncomfortable with the situation and you won't break the law.

- Should your boss persist, tell them you're not prepared to be put in a position that could jeopardize your career. Remember, if the deceit is uncovered, your boss may well try to cast the blame in every direction but their own. And you'll be right in the firing line.

> "Remember, if the deceit is uncovered, your boss may well try to cast the blame in every direction but their own. And you'll be right in the firing line".

- Get something in writing to make clear what you are being asked – and refusing – to do. That way if your boss tries to give you a hard time or punish you later, you have evidence of what has happened.

- You may feel what you are being asked to do is so serious that you should not only refuse but also blow the whistle on your boss. Only you know when this type of serious action is called for.

You're expected to do something you consider unethical

What if your boss wants you to tell lies to the board to get the department out of trouble, or to fiddle report sheets to make the figures look better? Or worse, suppose the organization expects you to dump contaminated waste at the local tip, or to contract out part of the manufacturing process to Far Eastern sweat shops employing child labour?

- If you are not personally expected to get involved in the dishonesty, you'll have to use your own judgement to decide when things are serious enough for you to take action.

- Once you decide to do something, go to your boss. Just as when you are asked to break the law, don't moralize or lecture them; simply tell them you are uncomfortable with the situation and feel you have to do something about it. This gives your boss a chance to stop doing whatever it is and you will let the matter rest.

- If your boss refuses to stop and you decide to take action, make sure you can prove your allegations of unethical behaviour. Your boss will very possibly deny it, and may well try to scapegoat you in some way. So secure your own position before going to whichever senior manager or department is appropriate.

- If the entire organization is involved in the unethical practice, you'll have to consider whether you are prepared to go on working for them.

Badly chaired meetings are wasting your time

There are few things more frustrating in this age of fast schedules and tight deadlines than strumming your fingers through long meetings that seem to be completely pointless, at least for you. But what can you do about it? To be honest, if you're not in the chair you're unlikely to make every meeting end on time, but there are still things you can do to speed the meeting up.

Sometimes you can see that a certain agenda item is only relevant to a few of the people at the meeting. If you're one of them, talk to the others and then contact the chairperson, offering to hold a mini-meeting in advance. That way instead of discussing the item – with everyone else throwing in their own opinions because they're there – you can simply present your results to the main meeting and move on to the next item.

One of the big delays to many meetings is that the group reaches an agreement but then continues the discussion without appearing to recognize the fact. The meeting ceases to be useful, and turns into some kind of group therapy session instead. The solution is simple. If the chairperson isn't doing their job, you'll have to do it for them. Be deferential so as not to put any backs up, and say to the chairperson: 'Am I right in thinking that we're all agreed on this?'

One of your options is to try to get out of part of the meeting. Ask the chairperson in advance if they can re-order the items on the agenda so you can leave partway through, having been present for all the items you need to contribute to. You'll have to generate a pretty good excuse, or everyone will soon be doing it with this kind of long-winded chairperson. But if you can arrange a meeting with an important client, for example, you'll have a good excuse.

You need to clear a blocked line of communication upwards

The bigger the organization, the more layers of management there will be above you. If there is an obstruction somewhere in this line of communication, you've got problems because you have no way of communicating with senior management.

The first thing to do is to identify the problem. You need to know which manager or director is obstructing you. You may well know this already. If not, start with your boss. If you ask them to pass a proposal or a request up the line, check with them later and see if they have.

If your boss isn't the problem, enlist their help to identify who is. They can check with their boss and so on – it won't be long before it becomes clear where the problem is. Bear in mind that the longer the line, the greater the chance that there's more than one weak point.

Next you need to find out whether your communications are being blocked deliberately or through inefficiency. If it isn't obvious, ask your boss to help you identify the cause. Has someone got it in for you or your department, or are they just unorganized?

If the problem is inefficiency, get your communication down in writing. Then keep reminding the person concerned until they pass it on. If you feel pushy doing this, disguise the reminder. For example, call them and say, 'I assume you'll be presenting my paper at Tuesday's meeting. I just called to check if you have any questions or need any supporting data to go with it?'

If your communications are being deliberately blocked, you may be able to talk directly to the person concerned. This is unlikely to work if they have a personal grudge against you, but maybe they're just blocking your proposal because they don't agree with it. Ask for a few minutes to talk to them, and say something like, 'I get the feeling you're not happy with my proposal. Can you tell me what's bothering you?' This kind of conversation might lead to you making a few adjustments to your proposal so that they are happy to pass it on.

With your boss's help, you can get your request or idea down in writing and then circulate it. Send it to the obstructive manager and to those above them, so they are not in a position to obstruct. If you can, find a good excuse for, effectively, going over their head. You might wait until they are away, and then explain that you needed a response urgently before you could finalize the budget for the exhibition.

Sometimes you can find a different route to senior management, which sidesteps your blockage. Suppose you have an idea for packaging your products differently that will make them cheaper to distribute. You work in distribution and can't get your distribution director to propose the idea. In that case, why not go to the marketing director instead? Packaging is a marketing issue after all. Bear in mind that going through a different route after your usual route has failed can look manipulative. So if you suspect your communication may be blocked, distribute your proposal or request through both routes at the same time.

You can't get senior management to listen to your idea

It may be that the lines of communication are blocked, in which case see page 139. If this isn't the problem, senior management can obviously hear your idea but they're not listening. So how do you get their attention? There are two basic ways to get through to management – by speaking to them, generally at meetings, or by putting what you have to say in writing.

Making your point at meetings

The key to this is to prepare in advance precisely what you want to say. The less you speak, the more people notice what you say. So don't waffle about every point on the agenda – save it for the one point where you really want to be heard. Apart from anything else, a chairperson in a hurry may cut you off if you've been taking a lot of the meeting's time already. They are very unlikely to cut you off if this is almost the first time you've spoken.

You don't want to recite from a script, but you do need to prepare pretty clearly what you're going to say. Keep it clear and succinct, don't wrap it up in justifications and explanations. If there's lots of relevant supporting facts and figures, put them on paper and hand round a copy for everyone to look at later. That way you don't have to waste senior managers' time at the meeting. There are some other points to consider:

- stick to two or three key points that illustrate your idea clearly. Try not to elaborate, and if people ask questions answer them briefly; don't ramble
- find a really well chosen example, anecdote or analogy that makes your point perfectly and succinctly
- speak clearly and without gabbling, and make eye contact as you speak.

Putting your ideas on paper

The other way to get the ear of senior management is to put your idea down in writing as a report, and to circulate it widely. A well written report, which carries a really good idea, is almost guaranteed to get noticed. You just need to make sure it's a really top-quality report. You can find books devoted to the subject of report writing, and you may find it useful to use one. But the most important points are:

- keep it short. Three or four pages is plenty for this kind of report, with appendices if you need them to hold any supporting data

- structure it clearly. Start by explaining why the idea is needed – what is it about the way the organization does things at present that needs improving? Then explain your idea and focus on the benefits to the organization

- set out the report professionally and readably. Don't cram great wodges of text on to the page; use plenty of headings and subheadings

- use *simple* diagrams or illustrations if they help to make your point more clearly

- even if your report is only three or four pages long, put a summary page at the front giving the key points. Your readers will read only this to begin with, and then decide if it seems worth reading the whole report

- put a cover page on the report with your name on it, and package it in a smart report folder.

You have to choose: keep your shareholders happy or look after your staff

Sometimes you're not given a choice in these situations. But, as a general rule, keep in mind that happy employees make for bigger profits. In the long term, therefore, doing the right thing by your staff will keep your shareholders happy too.

Fight for your team. It's what they need you for. You may not always win, but your team will still be happier for knowing you did your best for them.

CHAPTER 3

YOUR COLLEAGUES

Someone in a different department is making your life unbearable

When you have no common boss, how do you handle it? You'll need to use a technique called feedback. This involves talking to the other person about the problem, in a non-confrontational and constructive way. The 10 principles of feedback are very simple and can be applied to both personality and work-based issues. You can use feedback with colleagues, bosses or juniors.

1. Obviously you need to speak to the person in private, and at a time when neither of you is in a particular rush. Decide in advance what the key points you want to make are, and prepare ways of saying them that do not include:

   - exaggeration, such as 'you're always complaining'

   - judgements, such as 'you're hopeless at dealing with problems yourself'

   - labels, such as 'you're a whinger'.

2. When you speak to the person, focus on yourself and not them. Don't start sentences with, 'You make me feel . . .', try saying, 'I feel . . . when you . . .'. For example 'I feel frustrated when you don't give me the information I need.'

3. Explain why you feel this way: 'I can't meet my targets if I don't have the information to do the job.'

4. Now let the other person have their say. Listen to them, and show you're listening.

5. Be prepared to be criticized in turn. Maybe they see the problem as you always asking for information at the last minute. Is this a fair comment? You'll need to be very honest with yourself.

6. Focus on how they *behave*, not what they (in your view) *are*. So their behaviour may be unhelpful, but they are not automatically 'an obstructive person'.

7. Be prepared to quote actual instances wherever possible.

8. Be positive as well. Tell them when they have been helpful by giving you what you need promptly. Show them they *can* behave co-operatively.

9. Suggest a solution and see how the other person feels. This is very important; you can't change people's personalities, only their behaviour. So you must have an alternative behaviour in your mind that you are asking them to adopt. If you can't think of any solutions, you'd be better off not tackling the matter in the first place. Remember, you're not asking them to become a co-operative person – they can't necessarily do that – you're asking them (not in so many words) to be an unco-operative person who does manage to give you information promptly when you need it.

10. Listen to the other person's response and be prepared to compromise with them. (You may even learn something about how *you* appear to others, and be able to adapt your own behaviour and improve your performance.)

> "So their behaviour may be unhelpful, but they are not automatically 'an obstructive person'".

A colleague blows up at you in a meeting

I had a school friend whose father was a vicar. Mike was once leafing through the manuscript of one of his father's sermons, which had notes in the margin. He was highly amused to find that his father had written himself a note at one point that read, 'shout here, argument weak'.

In fact, Mike's father had registered an important technique, and one which many people use at meetings. They use force of personality because they haven't got force of argument. How often do people get emotional and angry when they have all the arguments on their side and they know they're going to win? They don't need to. So as soon as anyone starts to get angry, you know you've got them on the run.

Nevertheless, you don't actually want a colleague who spits blood at you. You will be far more popular with the meeting as a whole – and look far more like a good promotion prospect to your bosses – if you can keep the proceedings calm and pleasant as you politely win the battle.

And the technique for doing this is very simple. You remain calm yourself, don't respond with emotion but simply pick out the facts of what is being said and deal with those as you would if the person were talking calmly. If they keep haranguing you, just wait patiently until they run out of steam before you reply. A half-decent chairperson should intervene to let you speak but, if they don't, appeal to them by saying, calmly and politely, 'May I respond to that point?'

This might sound as though your opponent will get to do all the talking and you will be unable to put your case across. But it doesn't tend to work like

> "You will be far more popular with the meeting as a whole . . . if you can keep the proceedings calm and pleasant as you politely win the battle".

that. Not only will they look very silly if they're the only one losing control of their emotions, but they aren't likely to keep it up for very long if they don't get a heated response from you. They will burn out fast (after a brief period where you look cool and reasonable while they look like a three-year-old child), and the discussion will become calmer.

A colleague regularly turns meetings into a battlefield

There are two main reasons why anyone turns straightforward meetings into complex war zones, and you'll need to work out which is going on (it could be both):

- *Status battles:* whoever can prove themselves most senior reckons to be first in line for the next promotion. So everyone wants it to be *their* proposals that get agreed, and their arguments which win the day. All of this will make them appear more important than their colleagues.

- *Turf wars:* each manager has their own territory or department. And woe betide anyone who presumes to know more about production than the production manager, or attempts to take a prestigious project away from PR and get sales to run it instead. No one is prepared to give an inch of their territory, since the size and power of their department defines their personal clout.

Status battles

Broadly speaking your aim should be to win the argument – obviously – but to do it in a way that makes your colleague feel as positive and successful as possible. After all, you can afford to be generous over the details if you've won the battle.

Be pleasant

For a start, be as pleasant and friendly as you can, and ignore any attempts to goad you with criticisms or personal put-downs. You will only rile your opponent if you are arrogant, sarcastic or smug. The nicer you are, the less they will mind losing to you and the less they will fight the status battle alongside the practical argument you're debating.

Practise win/win negotiating

Win/win negotiating, as you may know, is the art of winning a negotiation in such a way that the other side feels they have also won. Give them as many brownie points as you can (while standing firm on the core issue), so they come away feeling like a winner and not a loser. So, for example:

- give them plenty of credit and praise – 'These figures Alex has come up with really are invaluable . . .' or 'I think the reason this solution will work is because Alex has such a strong team to carry it out . . .'

- make any minor concessions you can – 'I'm still certain that this is the right way to go. But I think Alex is right that we should delay until after the summer . . .'

- refer back to their previous successes – 'It's certainly possible to organize a project this size in the time if we had to. Look at the new computer system we put in last year; Alex's team organized that in only four months, and it went without a hitch.'

Turf wars

You're in big trouble if you tread on other people's toes in a meeting. Your colleagues no more want to share their expertize with you than Henry V wanted to share Normandy with the French. People are naturally territorial, and you forget it at your peril. So don't even think about putting forward ideas that entail reducing someone's reponsibilities unless you:

- suggest replacing them with other responsibilities (preferably ones that seem more prestigious)

- suggest that they are too important to do them, for example: 'If we handled the day-to-day paperwork for Mike, that would free up his team for more important tasks such as high-level negotiations with customers'.

Taking responsibilities away from people isn't the only way you can tread on their toes. No one likes it if you give the impression that you know more about their department or their area of expertize than they do. So don't make bald statements about other people's territories. Instead of saying, '92 per cent of our orders are repeat business', ask the sales manager, 'Jo, what percentage of our orders are repeat business?', or 'Mike, am I right in thinking that . . . ?' It's a matter of courtesy – after all, wouldn't you want them to do the same to you?

> "Your aim should be to win the argument – obviously – but to do it in a way that makes your colleague feel as positive and successful as possible".

A colleague in your team is no good but your boss can't see it

This is only an issue if your colleague's failings are making your working life more difficult. If this isn't the case, it's frankly none of your business. Frustrating . . . yes. But not your problem. However, if your own work is being compromised, you need to take action.

- Don't complain to your boss about the person involved. Focus on their work. Complaining about them personally isn't relevant, and if your boss can't see the problems it may look as if you have it in for them. Besides, it will understandably rile your colleague if they find out, and cause unpleasantness.

- When your colleague's work (or lack of it) creates a problem for you, let them know. For example, say to them: 'I need the figures from Brownes or I can't complete my report on time.' If this resolves things you don't need to take it further – your colleague is doing their job well enough, even if they need an occasional prompt. If it doesn't sort the problem out, *then* go to the boss. This way if your boss talks to the person concerned, you haven't gone behind their back – you gave them a chance to sort things out.

- When you go to the boss, don't mention the colleague's name – your focus should be on the work, not the person. So you simply say, for example, 'I have a problem. I'm supposed to deliver this report on Friday and I have all the information I need, except that I don't have the figures from Brownes. I can't complete the report without them.'

- Do this every time your work is compromised by your colleague. You don't have to mention their name (that might make it look personal), as your boss will soon realize where the real problem lies.

A colleague regularly puts emotional pressure on you

Have you ever heard any of the following? 'I'm going to be in a real mess if you don't help me out with this.' 'Just this once . . . I've been so under the weather lately and I just can't cope with this as well'. 'Please don't be unco-operative.' Emotional blackmail is a popular weapon for getting people to do whatever the blackmailer wants. Such people are playing on your guilt, or your desire to be popular, in order to manipulate you into doing things their way.

But there's one thing you need to know about emotional blackmail: it doesn't work on assertive people. If you find this situation tough, chances are that you're not as assertive as you could be. Emotional blackmailers learn to recognize assertive people and they stop using this insidious technique on them. So apply a bit of assertiveness and become impervious to this kind of manipulation. There are some steps you can take.

- Recognize emotional blackmail for what it is. As soon as you start to feel guilty about saying no, or emotionally uncomfortable about your response to someone, ask yourself 'Am I being emotionally blackmailed?' Once you're alert to the possibility, you'll have no trouble recognizing when it's happening.

- Tell yourself that emotional blackmail is not a fair, equal, adult behaviour and that you owe nothing to those who use it. If they're prepared to use such an underhand approach with you, you are quite entitled to respond by not giving in to it.

- Now simply stand your ground. If they persist, adopt the stuck record technique: 'I'm afraid I don't have the time' repeated firmly until they get

> "If you find this situation tough, chances are that you're not as assertive as you could be".

the message. Don't allow them to make you feel bad – it is they who are behaving unreasonably, not you.

- Challenging people directly over this technique can cause unpleasantness, but with some people you may find that you can say – with a joke and a laugh – 'Careful! That's starting to sound like emotional blackmail . . .' It pulls them up short. If they think you're getting wise to them they'll back off.

A colleague in your team is being manipulative

Good manipulators never leave any evidence; you can't actually *prove* that they've been manipulative. But you know it anyway. There's no point challenging them directly because they'll deny it. So make them feel that you want to help, not to point the finger.

- If they are manipulating a situation, they must have a reason. Think it through and work out what they are trying to achieve.

- Talk to them without accusing them of manipulation: 'I get the feeling that you'd like to run the ABC Ltd account. Is that right?'

- They will probably agree with you, but if they deny it give them reasons why you have this impression. 'I noticed at the meeting last Thursday that you highlighted one or two errors that had been made recently with the account. You don't normally focus on that kind of detail unless you have a particular interest in the subject so I concluded that you were probably interested in the ABC account.'

- Once the manipulator feels they can talk openly to you, without fear of accusations of manipulation, they will do so. After all, they are more likely to achieve their aim that way.

- Now you can have a balanced and reasonable discussion with them about the area where you feel you're being manipulated. Be careful not to be accusatory and to keep the discussion factual and unemotional. After all, they're entitled to want to run the same account you do. The problem is simply in their way of going about it.

- Now the issue is out in the open, you can go to your mutual boss if you can't find an agreement between you.

You are being sexually harassed by a colleague

It can be hard to define sexual harassment – what one person enjoys as flirting another may consider harassment. However, once you've made it clear that you consider a particular behaviour to be harassment, the person doing it should respect that. In the first instance, of course, this means you must tell the other person that you consider they are harassing you. Consider the following guidelines.

- Let them know how you feel about their behaviour and ask them to stop.

- If they don't stop, tell them you will make an official complaint against them. It is also wise at this point to start keeping a written record of their harassment.

- If this doesn't stop them, go ahead and make a complaint to your boss (if your own boss is harassing you, go to *their* boss). Many people worry that this will make matters worse; actually it almost never does. Anyone who persists in harassing you after you've made your feelings clear is going to

> "Once you've made it clear that you consider a particular behaviour to be harassment, the person doing it should respect that".

be pretty thick-skinned. A warning from the boss may be the only thing that will get through to them.

- If you can't get enough support to stop the harassment, you may decide to leave. If you have followed the company's grievance procedure and it has let you down, you may have sufficient grounds to sue for constructive dismissal.

You discover that one of your colleagues is breaking the rules

For a serious crime such as theft, you may feel obliged to report your colleague. But suppose it's a matter of minor pilfering or a small fiddle of the expenses? Or maybe they're taking time off when the boss thinks they're on company business? You can feel very compromised by this kind of rule-breaking. You don't want to be a snitch, but you don't want to be disloyal to the company either.

The best solution is to say to your colleague: 'I don't want to land you in it, but I know you're breaking the rules. I shan't say anything this time, but if I find you doing it again I shall feel obliged to tell the boss.'

> "You don't want to be a snitch, but you don't want to be disloyal to the company either".

CHAPTER 4

CUSTOMERS AND SUPPLIERS

You have an angry customer because you messed up

The first step in dealing with any angry customer, whatever the reason, is to listen while they get their anger out of their system. Sympathize with the problem with phrases such as, 'How frustrating for you,' or 'I can see how infuriating that must be'.

Once they have expressed their feelings, and realized that you are listening and sympathetic, they will calm down. At this point it is wise, as well as honest, to hold your hands up and admit your mistake by saying something like, 'I'm terribly sorry. I should have put the order through manually and I clean forgot. I do apologize, especially after it's caused you so much trouble'. This will take the wind out of their sails, not least because so few people actually admit to their mistakes.

> "So long as you offer to put things right in any reasonable way that suits the customer, they are likely to end up feeling very satisfied".

So long as you offer to put things right in any reasonable way that suits the customer, they are likely to end up feeling very satisfied. Not only have you resolved the problem, you've also been honest with them. It should reassure them that you're a good organization to do business with: everyone makes the occasional mistake, and at least you admit to it and put it right magnanimously.

Some people will advise you never to admit blame when dealing with customers in case they sue you. It may be wise to take legal advice if your mistake has cost them thousands, but in most cases they're not going to sue. If you've cost them just a few pounds, what's the problem? You ought to pay up, so there should be no question of suing. From a legal point of view, refusing to admit blame may sometimes be wise. From an ethical and customer relations standpoint, it is always better to admit your mistakes.

You have an angry customer because one of your team messed up

Handle this exactly as you would if it was you that had messed up (see page 162). You are responsible for your team, and you should carry the can. The customer doesn't need to know which individual in your team messed up; it's enough to know that it's *your* team. Don't ever try to pass the buck when speaking to a customer, tempting though it may seem to say, 'I'm afraid a junior member of my department made a mistake'.

You will obviously need to talk to the team member in question privately. However, you need to separate the mistake from the customer's reaction to it. If the customer overreacted wildly to a minor error of judgement or an understandable mistake, don't make a big deal of it with your team member just because the customer made a big deal of it with you. If you're angry and upset by your exchange with the customer, wait until you've calmed down before tackling the person who made the mistake.

> "You are responsible for your team, and you should carry the can".

You can't deliver on a promise to a customer

Whoops! If you can't deliver, you can't deliver. The important thing is to limit the damage, and there are two key ways to do this:

1. The most important thing is to give your customer as much notice as you possibly can. The later you tell them, the deeper the hole you land them in. Plenty of warning gives them time to find a contingency without it becoming a major issue. If you're not sure whether you can deliver but it's looking increasingly dodgy, you'll need to explain the situation before you know for certain whether you'll have to let them down. Then they can choose whether to take the risk or whether to find an alternative.

2. When you tell them, apologize profusely and let them know that you recognize how inconvenient it is for them. Then offer them whatever you can to make up for it. This might mean telling them you can deliver part of what they want, or they can have everything they want but later than they hoped or to a lower standard. Or you might say, 'I can't do this, but I can find you someone who can'.

A major customer threatens to go elsewhere unless you make concessions you can't afford

They say that they'll go to your manager/the top of your organization/the press. The answer is in the question here. If you really can't afford the concessions, you can't afford the customer and you're better off letting them go. Before you do, however, make sure that there really aren't any other concessions that would suit you both. If you can't drop your prices low enough, maybe they can pay in instalments or on other very good terms. If you can't deliver soon enough, perhaps you could deliver part of the order.

If there is no meeting ground, make sure you part on friendly terms. Don't tell them they'll regret changing supplier. That way, they may well come back to you. If they were bluffing to get you to make concessions, or if their new supplier lets them down, you want them to feel they can come back to you easily.

A disgruntled customer threatens to report you

They say that they'll go to your manager/top of your organization/the press. Let them. Presumably you've done nothing wrong, so you have nothing to worry about. Arguing with them will make it worse, and look as if you're running scared. If you say to them, 'If you feel you want to take it further, that's up to you,' it's more likely to deter them. After all, they were threatening in order to get a response from you. The tactic clearly hasn't worked so they may well abandon it.

If the customer threatens to go to someone internally, from your immediate boss to the MD, forewarn the manager concerned. They won't be too pleased if they get a call from a customer and look a fool because they don't have any of the facts. So brief them fully.

If by any chance you are at fault, you're still better off 'fessing up. It is better for your boss to hear it from you first than from an angry customer. (See also 'You have an angry manager because you messed up', page 162)

A customer is wrong

Sometimes a customer accuses you of doing something that you really haven't done. In fact, maybe their subsequent problems have arisen because they failed to give you their full address, or sign the cheque. So what do you do when they complain? Is the customer really *always* right?

- You need to listen to their complaint and sympathize with their problem just as you would if the complaint were justified. You can still say, 'How frustrating!' or 'I can see that must have put you in a difficult position,' without admitting blame.

- Tactfully explain what has caused the problem, but don't make them feel stupid or they could get defensive. Avoid words and phrases such as 'fault' or 'you should have . . .'. Give them an excuse for their mistake. For example, 'Our delivery terms are 28 days unless you specify express delivery. I know how easy it can be to overlook that sort of thing, especially when you're in a hurry.'

- Let them feel their point is valid, without accepting blame. Say for example, 'Maybe we should print our delivery terms on the order form as well as on the terms and conditions. I'll suggest that to the department concerned.'

- Don't offer refunds or replace items just to calm a customer down, in case it implies that you were at fault. This might be an unwise precedent. However, if you really want to do something, describe it as a gesture of appreciation for bringing their problem to your attention.

You know one of your customers is lying to you

You get them occasionally: customers who frequently claim, for example, that the goods arrived faulty or damaged when you know for a fact that they didn't. Whatever you do, don't bother arguing. You've got two options:

1. give the customer the benefit of the doubt

2. stop supplying them and ask them to go elsewhere.

You've already got a dishonest customer. If you argue with them, you'll have an angry, dishonest customer – and that's worse. They may spread rumours or damaging gossip about your organization. So don't fall out with them.

The other trap to avoid is changing your systems in order to try and combat their dishonesty. You could inconvenience all your honest customers, and make your own lives more complicated, just for the sake of a customer who doesn't deserve that kind of effort. So if you don't want to put up with it, just drop the customer.

An important customer demands more of your time than you can spare

If you have a very talkative customer who engages you in long-winded conversations, you need to find a way to get the information you need from them and then terminate the conversation without upsetting them. You can't keep interrupting them without sounding rude, so you need to interrupt yourself.

It may sound strange, but it makes sense really. You need to get a word in, but to do it by joining their conversation rather than deflecting it. Once you're in, *then* you can change the subject, like this: 'I quite agree, the traffic's getting silly on the North Circular these days. By the way, when do you need these delivered by?'

Frequent callers

There's another kind of demanding customer, too: the one who's on the phone 10 times a day with endless minor queries. You can't avoid this customer altogether, and you'll offend them if you try. You just need to get them to be less of a nuisance:

- If someone's calling several times a day, tell them the first time they call that you're very busy at the moment and you want to wait until you can give them your full attention. Ask if you can call back at the end of the day. They can save all their questions until you ring back, and you have only one call all day, at a time of your choosing.

> "You can't avoid this customer altogether, and you'll offend them if you try. You just need to get them to be less of a nuisance".

- Put your voicemail on or have someone field your calls. You do have to talk to this customer sometimes, however, so don't wind them up by taking ages to call back. Once they learn they can trust you to call back the same day – albeit at the end of the day – they'll start to feel happier about leaving messages.

- If the customer is on email, ask them to email you instead of calling. Explain that you prefer to have everything in writing so you can be sure you have all the details, and you don't forget to follow anything up. Now you can deal with the queries at a time that suits you. You may have to speak to them occasionally but, again, you can choose the time.

A good and previously reliable supplier lets you down badly

In the short term, you need to find another supplier. The question is whether in the long term you should change to a new supplier or whether you should give this one another chance. In the end it's your decision, but here are some considerations to take into account:

- Why did they let you down? Is it something they should have foreseen and avoided? Or was it the kind of freak problem that no one could have anticipated?

- How did they let you down? Did they give you as much warning as possible that trouble was brewing? Did they sound suitably concerned at letting you down? Did they do anything to try to mitigate the damage?

- Have they ever let you down before? Have there been other minor incidents, or is this the first problem in years?

- Why were you using them in the first place? What is it that makes them better than other suppliers?

- Could you find another supplier as good as them in all the essentials – price, quality, reliability, service and so on? Shop around and see what else is available.

By the time you've thought through all these questions, you should be in a position to decide whether to stick with this supplier or not. And there's one other thing you can do – monitor the service and quality you get from whichever supplier you use as a replacement (assuming you find another supplier for this order). This should give you an idea of whether it's worth moving your contract.

You have a PR crisis on your hands

Everyone loves a drama – except perhaps the people caught up in it. Inevitably, then, many crises will attract the attention of the press. They gather like hyenas around the kill, each hungry to get first bite at the story. And not only do you have to deal with the crisis itself but you also have to cope with the press, who will be ready at any moment to turn on you if you make a wrong move.

The press can be either a blessing or a curse in a crisis, and the balance can lie in how you handle them. Of course, sometimes the press are on your side from the start. If your buildings have been damaged by severe weather, or a lorry has careered off the road straight through your shop window, you have the sympathy of the media from the outset.

But the press always want someone to blame, and all too often they will pick on you. If you're making redundancies, if you've polluted the river that runs past the factory or if an accident has been caused by faulty equipment then they'll be sniffing round for evidence to pin the blame on you.

So what can you do? The good news is that there is a wealth of advice, derived from the experience of thousands of organizations over many years. There *are* ways to handle the press (and other media) that will at least minimize the damage and, at best, turn their attitude around to one of support for your case. So below are the key rules for handling a PR crisis.

Keep in touch

Tell the press what's going on right from the start. Keep them sweet by holding press conferences; don't wait to be asked. Get outside the front gates and tell them what is happening. The more information you give them, the less they will need to dig the dirt to get a decent story. Don't wait until you've resolved the crisis – keep them posted from the moment they turn up asking questions.

It's no good keeping the press informed if you don't also keep your own people posted. Otherwise disgruntled staff, who are being kept in the dark, may well decide to pass on to the press their own outdated or misunderstood version of the facts.

Be honest

Remember Richard Nixon? If you get caught lying, you're done for. It's *never* worth the risk.

Honesty can actually be a disarmingly smart policy. Many years ago, the BBC accidentally double booked two key political figures to give one of the prestigious Reith lectures. One had to be cancelled, of course, and the press were full of how and why he had been snubbed. The Director General of the BBC adopted a simple but ingenious approach when questioned by the press. He just said: 'It was a cock up, OK?' He was open, honest and wrong-footed the press completely. We all have cock ups from time to time, and the press understand that as well as anyone.

Keep it simple

There are three rules to remember to keep things simple. (I know there should only really be one. Sorry.) First: the press don't know your organization or your industry as well as you do, and they want to print a clear, simple story for their readers. So don't confuse them with unnecessary details, jargon or background information they don't want. Just keep your

> "The press can be either a blessing or a curse in a crisis, and the balance can lie in how you handle them".

message uncluttered. If they ask for more, give it to them if you can. But don't volunteer it.

The second rule of keeping your story simple is to make sure you have only one spokesperson if you possibly can. Otherwise there is a danger that they may contradict each other. One single point of communication means one single, consistent voice.

And the third rule is: never speculate. This simply adds to the confusion. Speculation may be reported as fact – it often is. So if you're asked to guess at the cause of the chemical leak, how many redundancies there are likely to be or when the building will be operational again, politely decline to comment. Or just say, 'I don't know'.

So, to recap, the three rules of keeping it simple are:

1. don't give more information than you need to

2. have a single, consistent message delivered by a single spokesperson

3. never speculate.

Get your priorities right

You will horrify readers, listeners or viewers if you start to talk about the financial cost of this disaster when people have been killed or injured. Likewise, they aren't concerned about your faulty equipment when you've just killed all the wildlife in a 10 mile stretch of the river. So talk about the crisis in the light of the public's priorities. These are:

1. people

2. environment

3. property

4. financial implications.

Be aware how things look to other people

Be aware of what the public perception of your crisis handling will be. It's not enough to be right – you have to be *seen* to be right. Suppose a press story breaks reporting that many supermarket eggs are infected with salmonella, and there is a slight risk of serious illness. You are an egg producer. If you react by insisting that there is no danger at all, people will just think, 'They would say that, wouldn't they?'

There may indeed be no danger – or there may be. It doesn't matter. What matters is that people will *think* you are trying to cover up the facts for your own ends; that you're prepared to lie to people about their health rather than lose profits. So consider how your version of events, which people will

> "Be aware of what the public perception of your crisis handling will be. It's not enough to be right – you have to be *seen* to be right".

consider potentially very biased, will look. It is better to say that you are very concerned about the health scare over eggs – you have no evidence that there is any risk at all, but you're taking action to find out the facts as fast as possible. Support any research – maybe donate funds to it – and invite inspectors to check out your operation. Say you would welcome official guidelines on how your organization can remove any risk, and generally be seen to be taking the action the public wants, not just paying lip service to it.

Never 'no comment'

What do you think when you hear an interviewee say 'no comment', or when a report says that 'the company declined to comment'? You think they're guilty, don't you? You reckon they've got something to hide. That's what everyone thinks. And it's what they'll think about you, if you say 'no comment'. So don't. If there's nothing you can tell them, it's better to say, 'I'm afraid I don't have any more information at the moment'.

Be positive

If you seem worried or down beat in interviews, people will assume you're in trouble. If you come across as angry they will take a dislike to you. People will read a great deal into your attitude, so make sure it is always friendly and positive, especially when you're talking to the broadcast media. If people have suffered, it doesn't do to look too cheerful about it, of course. But you can still be open and courteous. Make sure you show sympathy for any victims of the disaster, whether or not you accept responsibility.

Be friendly

The press are only doing their job. If you want them on your side, you need to accept this and not hold grudges against them. Let them use the phone, and the cafeteria (if it can cope), and give them a warm room if you can spare one and the weather's atrocious outside.

Always treat the press politely and with respect, whether or not they show you the same courtesy. Be as helpful as you can in giving them press packs, background information or whatever else they ask for.

Get your friends on your side

If the press are against you, recruit people outside the company who will speak on your behalf. Satisfied customers, trade association contacts, suppliers, ex-employees . . . anyone who the press will be interested to talk to and whom you can rely on to back you up. They will assure the press that your safety standards are exemplary, that you're a great company to work for, that you are known for your reliability or whatever it is you need said. Outsiders always have more credibility than insiders.

Go the extra mile

If you've made a mistake, or are believed to have made a mistake, do everything you can to put it right. Even if people blame you for the crisis itself, don't give anyone an excuse to complain about your response to it. Do even more than you have to. Give people extra time off, replace their damaged property without quibble and better than it was before, pay to clean up the river *and* fund a new wildlife reserve along its banks. Show that you're sorry you messed up, but you genuinely want to make everything better.

You may remember a few years ago a cross channel ferry ran aground on a sandbank. Due to the vagaries of the tide it was a day or so before they could float it off again. Meantime everyone was stuck on board. But the ferry company and the crew leapt into action as soon as the disaster struck. They kept everyone informed, refunded the cost of the tickets, gave away all the free food and drink they could and generally bent over backwards to make up for the discomfort and inconvenience.

When the ferry finally docked, the press were waiting to interview the passengers as they disembarked. But much to their disappointment (I should imagine), they couldn't find a single passenger who had a bad word to say about the ferry operator. They all insisted, 'It was just bad luck, and they looked after us beautifully'.

Remember, you don't have to deal with very many crises (thank heaven), but the press deal with them for a living. They are bound to be smarter than you at it, so don't try to fool them – they'll make you look the fool. Just play it straight, honest and open.

> "Remember, you don't have to deal with very many crises (thank heaven), but the press deal with them for a living".

CHAPTER 5

YOU

You've made a bad decision and you're asked to justify it

If you try to justify this decision, you'll simply make things worse. Remember: when you're in a hole, stop digging. If it's not too late you may be able to change the decision, or make some other change that alleviates the problems the bad decision has caused. For example, if your decision means you can't meet the deadline for a project perhaps you can find a way to move the deadline.

Unless you can remedy the problems before anyone notices, however, it is far better to admit to making a bad decision than to insist it was a good decision and try to justify it. You can disarm people with an honest admission that you've made a mistake, followed by an apology. Just remember:

- be honest
- don't try to blame the bad decision on anyone else – even if others were involved too
- if you're talking to your boss, show you recognize where you made a misjudgement and have learned from it.

Having admitted to making a poor decision, you need to show that you can be positive about putting things right. So you need to have a plan of action to follow on from the results of your decision. Instead of justifying the bad decision, therefore, you are in effect saying: 'I made a bad decision, and I'm

> "Having admitted
> to making a poor
> decision, you need to
> show that you can be
> positive about putting
> things right".

sorry. But here's what we can do to limit the damage . . .' and then justify this follow up decision. You can offer a choice of actions or put things right. Either way, show how you can stop the mistake happening again.

Someone reneges on a promise but you didn't get it in writing

The first thing to do here is to doublecheck that you really don't have a record of the promise. Is there an email still in the system anywhere with reference to it? Have you kept any notes that refer to it? If not, can you be quite sure it is the other party, and not you, who has misremembered the agreement?

If you're certain about the promise and you really don't have any record of it, your next option is to appeal to the other person's better nature. Many people will respond positively, or at least work out a compromise. Don't put them on the defensive by accusing them of cheating you, or they're hardly likely to co-operate. Tell them there has been a misunderstanding and ask them to help put it right.

If the other person is adamant that they won't budge, you may be able to go over their head. Whether they are a colleague, a supplier or a customer, an appeal to their boss can put things right. Again, however, don't put their back up by telling tales of them trying to con you. Find a tactful way to suggest that they may have misunderstood you.

In the end, if you simply can't get the response you want, you'll have to live with the consequences. Consider whether you want to do business with this person again; if you do, you'll certainly want to make sure you get everything in writing next time. (See also 'You know one of your customers is lying to you', page 169.)

It's discovered that you haven't told the truth

Now here's a tough situation you should never have got into. But it can happen to the best of us occasionally. We tell what we feel is a little white lie, and usually we get away with it. When we get caught, however, the very fact that we lied often looks far worse than whatever it was we were trying to hide.

Honesty is always the approach to take. Don't ever compound the lie or you could end up in big trouble simply for your dishonesty, regardless of how insignificant the lie itself might be. You undermine your own trustworthiness, and make it very difficult for others to work with you. So why did you lie?

- *By accident:* it may be that you weren't really lying, so much as guessing wrong. When this happens, admit that you believed you were telling the truth but you hadn't checked. Apologize.

- *To protect someone:* admit what you were doing, whether or not you feel you can disclose who you were trying to protect.

- *You hoped it was true:* suppose your boss asks you how far you've got with the report that's due to be delivered on Friday. You haven't started it but, because you know you'll have it done in time, you say you're about halfway through. Your boss says, 'Good, because I need whatever you've done for this morning's meeting. Please can you hand it over?' You'll have to 'fess up, apologize and explain why you lied. In this case, you might explain that you knew it would be finished in time, and you didn't want your boss to worry unnecessarily that it wouldn't get done.

- *Intentionally:* this kind of premeditated lie is often more serious. Perhaps you gave false qualifications when you applied for this job, and it's just come to light. Apologize as always, and explain why you did it. For example, 'I knew I could do this job and I really wanted it. But I was worried you wouldn't appoint me if you knew I hadn't been to university.' Show that you're sorry and that you understand that it was wrong. If you have told any other lies, admit to them now (such as 'I'm afraid my references were false too'). If they are exposed later your employer's trust in you will be completely shattered.

> "Don't ever compound the lie or you could end up in big trouble simply for your dishonesty, regardless of how insignificant the lie itself might be".

You have to take a really close decision

Some decisions are pretty obvious. Some aren't so clear, but then it's not that important. And then there are the decisions that are really tough. It's a close call, and it matters that you get it right.

It's easy to defer this kind of decision, but that really doesn't help. You need to go through the decision making process properly, and then take the decision firmly:

- Collect all the relevant facts and information that you can.

- Consult anyone whose input may be helpful. Remember that you don't have to follow the advice you're given – this is *your* decision – you just need to listen to it.

- Think through the options, and be as open-minded and creative as you can. Suppose you have to make someone redundant. It doesn't have to be a straight either/or choice. Maybe you could offer two people a jobshare. Maybe you could shift responsibilites and make someone who wasn't on your original list redundant instead. There are usually more options than are initially obvious.

- Evaluate each of the options. There are various ways of doing this that will help you to reach a decision. Try some or all of them:

  1. think through the worst-case and best-case scenarios

  2. consider the likelihood of each of these scenarios actually happening

  3. think through the consequences of each decision for the organization, the department, the people involved, the budget, the production schedule and yourself

> "Think through the options, and be as open-minded and creative as you can".

4. list the pros and cons

5. ask yourself what you would regret most if you do or don't take each option.

- Rule out as many options as you can on the basis of your evaluation.

You have now been through every process necessary to take this decision, so you'd better take it. Usually it's obvious by this stage, even if it's simply the least worst option of several unsatisfactory ones. If there's honestly nothing to choose between two options, you might as well toss a coin. Honestly. At least you'll have a decision, and if there's nothing to choose between after all that how will you ever have a better method of deciding?

Finally, whatever decision you take, once it's made you must commit yourself to it totally. Even if you made it reluctantly, you must communicate it and follow it through with conviction and confidence.

You have vastly more work than time

Everything's important and people are depending on you. Here's a catch-22. You're going to have to clear some time to deal with this problem. It may seem impossible, but you can always clear time if it's important enough. Suppose the MD's secretary phoned to say that the MD wanted to see you for two hours tomorrow morning before they make their final decision on who to promote. You'd find the time for that, wouldn't you?

Once you make the decision that you have to tackle this problem, you'll find a few hours. Come in very early one morning, or cancel a meeting or appointment that you don't really need to go to and use the time you've freed up.

So what are you going to do with this time? You need to be very disciplined and go through all your work and sort it out. Don't get distracted into dealing with any of it during this session – you can do that later. For now, you need to organize your work and, essentially, get rid of as much of it as you possibly can. Be very ruthless or this process won't work:

- Bin everything that you can. Anything non-essential will have to go. All those papers to read and letters to write. If your business or your department can survive without them getting done, don't do them.

- Say no to everything you possibly can. Make a list of meetings, appointments and requests that you can probably get out of, and do it. Email your polite refusals if you can – it saves getting embroiled in long conversations or pressure to get you to change your mind. The more time you can free up this way, the more time you have to deal with the work you do still have to keep. Remember that the more notice you give people, the less of a problem they have if you cancel an engagement. So clear your diary well ahead.

- Delegate anything you can. Just remember that it's unreasonable to offload three weeks work onto someone who is already snowed under, and then ask them to complete it in the next three days. The more people you can delegate the work to, the more you can offload.

You should now have a lot less work in front of you. On the other hand, you should also have cleared a lot more time to do it in. What's left, however, really needs to be done. It's all important and you'll be letting people down if you don't do it.

- The key thing is to prioritize. Organize the remaining tasks in order of how important they are. If they are both important *and* urgent, do them first. If they are important but not urgent, you still need to get them done (not doing such tasks is how you arrived here in the first place).

- Schedule these tasks into your diary – you may want to come into work an hour or two early for the next few days to work through everything. Be extremely strict with yourself about keeping to time. Clock-watch constantly. Ban interruptions. If you have an hour for a certain task, make sure you don't go over time.

- Make a rule that you won't go home until all the day's tasks are done. Schedule yourself to leave by about 6p.m. each evening (it won't help if you become exhausted and overstressed), but don't leave until you're up-to-date. That way, you can't get behind again.

- If you have tasks scheduled in your diary, that means the time is not available for anything else. So don't let your diary fill up with anything else non-essential. Keep saying no politely, or declining appointments and meetings that are unnecessary. And keep binning or delegating everything you can. That way, you only have to fit the very top priorities into your schedule – like the MD wanting to see you tomorrow morning about that promotion.

"If you have tasks scheduled in your diary, that means the time is not available for anything else. So don't let your diary fill up with anything else non-essential".

You are promoted over former colleagues

This can be tricky to begin with, but if you handle it right you should soon settle into your new role. The important thing is not to put their backs up by lording it over them and playing the big boss. This can be tempting as a way of imposing your authority when you fear they won't respect it, but actually it will backfire.

If you are confident in yourself, you shouldn't have a problem. Your boss wouldn't have promoted you if they didn't believe that your colleagues respected you, now would they? So adopt a supportive management style and trust your own ability to command respect (see also 'Your team complain that they don't like your management style,' page 19).

The only other difficulty you may encounter is that your ex-colleagues might try to take advantage of the fact that you were recently one of their peers. They may think they can get away with lax behaviour or performance because you're all mates together. As soon as there is any sign of this, nip it in the bud. Deal with any issues of this kind promptly and firmly (see also 'You have to discipline a team member who is also a friend', page 96).

You are promoted over people older than you

This is only a problem if your new team see it as a problem. In essence, you're dealing with prejudice here. It's understandable that older people might feel resentful at having a young upstart put in charge of them, but if you handle it right they'll soon forget your age.

- Recognize that you'll never change this kind of prejudice, so there's no point trying. Your aim is to ensure that if your team thinks young managers are no good, you're an exception to this.

- Work very hard to show them that you deserve the job on your own merits, and your lack of age doesn't inhibit your ability in any way.

- Never give any hint that you consider it an issue. Don't brag about landing such a good job so young, or tell them that if they'd worked harder they could be where you are now.

If you're a good manager, and you follow these guidelines, you should soon find that your team stop noticing your relative ages. If anyone's prejudice is a real problem, you'll need to talk to them privately about it, following the guidelines for feedback (see page 146).

You are promoted over someone who really resents you

The most common reason for this is that the person concerned was after the promotion and resents the fact it was you that won it. When this happens, it's a good idea to call the person in for a private meeting as soon as you start your new job. If it's too late for that now, it's still worth doing it as soon as possible. Here are some guidelines on how to tackle such a meeting:

• Tell them that you know they wanted the job too. Don't justify your promotion – 'It was a fair fight' or 'I'm more experienced than you' – but acknowledge how they must feel. Tell them something like, 'It's a difficult situation. I know how I'd feel if you'd got the job.'

• Let them know that you're sure they won't let it get in the way of your relationship. As one of the most experienced and able members of the team (presumably they are if they were up for the job too) you're hoping they'll be there to give you plenty of support while you find your stride.

• If it's already getting in the way of your relationship (if you didn't have this conversation at the start) use feedback (see page 146) to help resolve the problem.

• Give them a particular area of responsibility or a challenge that they will really enjoy. This shows you won't be prejudiced against them or feel threatened by them, and will help to offset any feelings of lost pride at not getting the job themselves.

• You need to establish your authority over your new team, but be very careful not to be heavy-handed about discipline or dealing with mistakes, especially with this person. (And since you need to treat everyone equally, that will go for the whole team.)

See also 'You are promoted over former colleagues', page 192, 'You are promoted over people older than you', page 193, 'Your team complain that they don't like your management style', page 19.

You have to choose between work and family

In many jobs work and family don't clash persistently, but every so often a serious conflict arises. For example, you're supposed to be away at an exhibition and it's your 10th wedding anniversary. Or you're all working flat out for the forthcoming launch when your father is taken into hospital seriously ill. You can't meet both commitments, so what do you do?

The first thing to do is talk to your boss and see if they are prepared to help you accommodate your personal commitments. Many bosses – all the considerate ones – will do their best. If your boss either can't or won't help, you'll have to decide who to let down – work or home.

Sometimes the family commitment is so strong you feel you have no choice. If it's more important to you than work then do it. This often arises where death or serious illness are involved.

But what if the family pull is strong but not essential – being there for an important birthday or anniversary, for example? Think through the worst possible scenario of letting down either work or home. Will you get a ticking off from your boss? Will you miss out on a project you really want to work on? Will you get sacked? If you decide the other way, will you feel guilty but nothing worse? Will your child be deeply hurt? Will your partner divorce you? By thinking through the consequences of your options, you should be able to arrive at a decision. Good luck.

Your work encroaches on your personal time

This can be caused by a boss who expects you to work longer hours than the job is supposed to entail. If this is the case, see page 117. However, sometimes the hours the work is supposed to take get in the way. This most often happens when your personal circumstances change. Frequent travelling was fine before you had kids, but not any more. Long hours used to be fine, but now your elderly mother is living with you it's a problem being home so late.

You need to talk to your boss – but you need to be realistic, too. Come up with suggestions for changing your working hours without compromising the organization – you took this job, after all, and you made a commitment to work those hours. Here are some possibilities that might work for you, or which might spark you off on some alternative ideas:

* start work earlier in the mornings, and leave earlier in the evenings

* work through lunch and leave an hour early

* combine both the above ideas – arrive early and work through lunch to buy an even earlier finish time

* work from home some days

* work from home for a couple of days to compensate after a business trip

* make sure business trips are always midweek, and never involve flying out or back at weekends

* increase your holiday entitlement instead of taking a salary rise

* go part time, or at least cut your hours and your pay accordingly.

Now go to your boss with all the ideas you have that you feel would work for you. If you're good at your job, and your boss has any sense, they'll want to co-operate rather than lose you.

If you get no joy from your boss, you'll have to decide whether the job is worth the personal sacrifice, or whether you'd be happier changing jobs and working more convenient hours. Only you can make this decision.

You feel you can't cope with the pressure

If you're getting seriously stressed at work, you need to do something about it. And the sooner you take action, the easier it will be to ease the pressure. Not only do you need to be less pressured for your own benefit, but the department and the organization also need you to be happy and relaxed. That way, you will work better and most likely stay longer with the company.

If things are really getting on top of you, talk to your boss. Explain clearly what the problems are, and also the symptoms. They are far more likely to recognize the need to take action if you point out that you've missed a couple of deadlines lately, or you made a mistake last week that could have had serious repercussions. Let them know that it is the pressure of work that is causing you to lose concentration and enthusiasm.

If things get too bad, your doctor can sign you off for a while. However, that's not the ideal solution for you or your boss, so here are a few alternatives that may help. Pick and choose those which you feel will help ease the pressure for you, and talk to your boss about those that need their approval:

- take a few days off
- work at home for a few days
- change your work patterns so you always spend a day or two a week at home
- go into work later or leave earlier – on either a permanent or a temporary basis, whichever you need
- move to a quieter/less isolated/more isolated/less cramped desk or office – whichever will help

- take a proper lunch break every day and spend it walking in the park, reading or even having a nap

- go on a time management course to help you organize your work and your time better

- clear your backlog of work (see page 189). Take a day or two out, by arrangement with your boss, to do this

- take lots of five minute breaks, especially breaks from the computer screen.

There are also more personal steps you can take, which will have a long-term impact on your stress levels. If you can relax properly away from work, you'll get a lot less stressed when you're at work. Again, everyone's different so choose the ones that help you:

- spend more time socializing if you're isolated at work – or less time socializing if you're getting too tired

- switch to decaffeinated coffee

- take up a relaxing or stress-busting activity such as yoga, meditation or a martial art

- resolve any sleeping problems. The most useful thing is to have a routine time to go to bed and to get up every day, regardless of how you sleep. Don't lie in at weekends because you've had a bad night, and don't go to bed very early because you're tired. This way, you will train your body into a sleep routine. Within a week or two you should find you sleep better

- learn to relax on the hoof by breathing more efficiently. Close your eyes and take a few deep breaths using your diaphragm to breathe in and out.

> "Whatever you do, don't try to carry on regardless when you're struggling to cope".

Whatever you do, don't try to carry on regardless when you're struggling to cope. It may work if you know things will be fine after Friday's big presentation, but if the problem is ongoing it won't go away until you address it. So do it now.

More power to your
[## business-]

Even at the end there's more we can learn. More that *we* can learn from your experience of this book, and more ways to add to *your* learning experience.

For who to read, what to know and where to go in the world of business, visit us at **business-minds.com**.

Here you can find out more about the people and ideas that can make you and your business more innovative and productive. Each month our e-newsletter, *Business-minds Express*, delivers an infusion of thought leadership, guru interviews, new business practice and reviews of key business resources directly to you. Subscribe for free at

▶ **www.business-minds.com/goto/newsletters**

Here you can also connect with ways of putting these ideas to work. Spreading knowledge is a great way to improve performance and enhance business relationships. If you found this book useful, then so might your colleagues or customers. If you would like to explore corporate purchases or custom editions personalised with your brand or message, then just get in touch at

▶ **www.business-minds.com/corporatesales**

We're also keen to learn from your experience of our business books – so tell us what you think of this book and what's on *your* business mind with an online reader report at business-minds.com. Together with our authors, we'd like to hear more from you and explore new ways to help make these ideas work at

▶ **www.business-minds.com/goto/feedback**

[www.business-minds.com
www.financialminds.com]

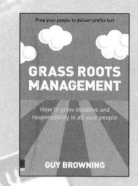

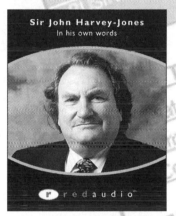

Beat Your Goals

The definitive guide to personal success

David Molden
0273 65670 8

It's about setting goals that have true meaning and how to use all the available resources to become a serial high achiever. It's about removing the hurdles to achieve your aspirations. It's about turning goals into reality!

Coach Yourself

Anthony Grant
1843 04013 1

Imagine waking up tomorrow morning and your life being exactly how you want it to be. This book will help you help yourself get there. Coaching is a powerful and effective management tool. Imagine the power of knowing how to coach yourself.

Real Coaching and Feedback

JK Smart
0273 66328 3

"Reading this book is like somebody switching on the light – suddenly you can see for yourself what you need to do differently. It doesn't tell you what to do, because frankly it's going to be different for everybody and one size doesn't fit all. It triggers the thoughts that let you work it out for yourself. So you create your own solutions, instead of your own problems. And that actually makes you feel good as well as getting the results you want."
A Real Manager

Please visit our website at:

www.business-minds.com